SYMPHONY

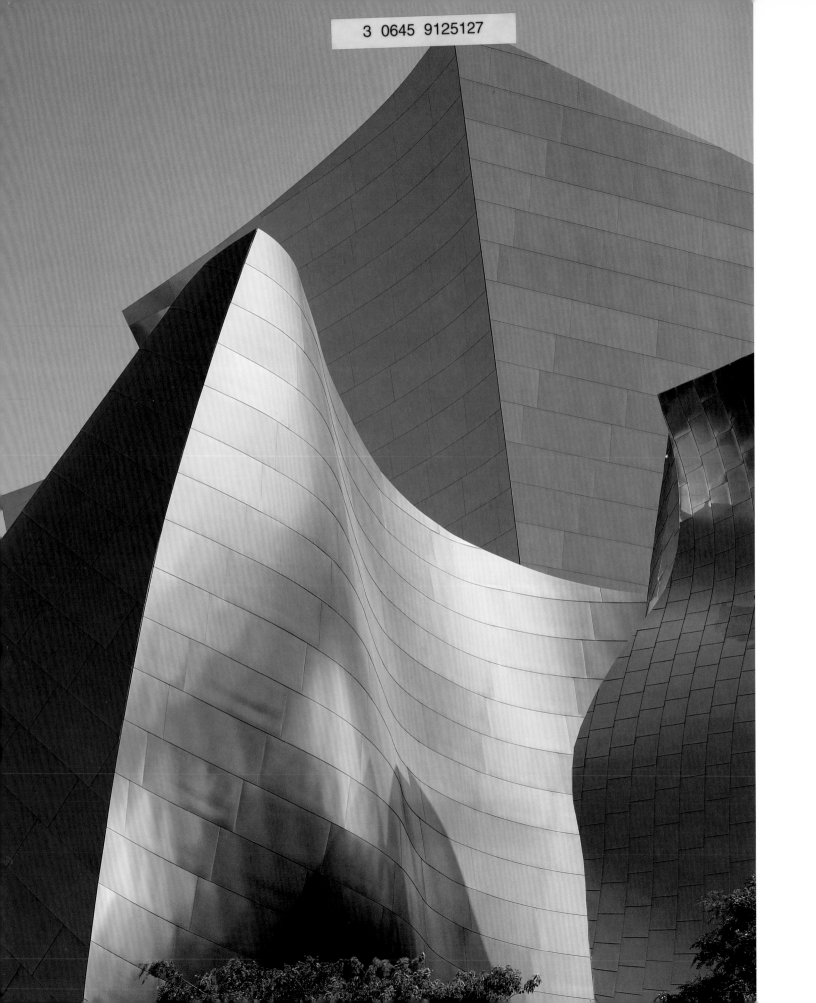

SYMPHONY: FRANK GEHRY'S WALT DISNEY CONCERT HALL

preface by DEBORAH BORDA
introduction by FRANK GEHRY

with essays by
RICHARD KOSHALEK
and DANA HUTT,
CAROL MCMICHAEL REESE,
MICHAEL WEBB,
and ESA-PEKKA SALONEN

photography by GRANT MUDFORD

HARRY N. ABRAMS, INC., PUBLISHERS
IN ASSOCIATION WITH
THE LOS ANGELES PHILHARMONIC

TABLE OF CONTENTS

PREFACE

This book celebrates the completion of a long-awaited project: Walt Disney Concert Hall, new home of the Los Angeles Philharmonic. You will read in these pages the story of the vision, creativity, and effort behind the realization of this building. It is a roller coaster of a story, but the ending, as evidenced in the remarkable photographs of Grant Mudford, is triumphant.

I cannot imagine an orchestra better suited to the daring of Frank Gehry. The Los Angeles Philharmonic is a special orchestra that deserves a hall as wonderful and adventuresome as the building created for it by Gehry and his team. It was a privilege for me to work on this project, and an epiphany to share in the extraordinary collaboration between Frank Gehry and Esa-Pekka Salonen. Gehry's building has been an invitation to dream, and a challenge to develop in new and innovative ways.

We at the Los Angeles Philharmonic see the opening of Walt Disney Concert Hall as a marvelous beginning. The hall will dramatically alter the way we experience music. It will be transformative, not only for the Philharmonic, but also for the city of Los Angeles. We see the orchestra as a convener of intellectual life in our city. At Walt Disney Concert Hall, we will present the greatest musical artists of our time; with our many cultural partners, we will be able to enrich these programs with a variety of symposia, panel discussions, exhibitions, talks, and other communal activities. In these pages Frank Gehry is quoted as saying that the hall is a "living room for the city." We intend to fill it with the full spectrum of life—with living music.

While there were many, many people involved in this project—an entire city, in fact—there is a special group of people without whom it would never had been accomplished. This book is dedicated to them: Lillian Disney, who provided the generous gift that set this project in motion; Diane Disney Miller, who supported the project with unfaltering focus; Ernest Fleischmann whose vision was inspiring and steadfast; and Eli Broad, Richard Riordan, and Andrea Van de Kamp, whose leadership and tireless efforts on behalf of this building resulted in a triumph for the city of Los Angeles.

DEBORAH BORDA
Executive Director, Los Angeles Philharmonic

INTRODUCTION

I believe that the design of Walt Disney Concert Hall suggests music, and I hope that when people attend concerts in the hall, their eyes will wander through the shapes of the building and find that what they see harmonizes with the music they're listening to. In my work I have always used art and music as a kind of inspirational motor. When I get stuck, I go look at paintings or listen to music. I find music in particular reassuring, and in many ways it just gets me going. It's energizing. And so the connection between architecture and music has always seemed natural to me.

My mother used to take me to concerts when I was a child, and I suppose that's where my interest in classical music began. All through college I had close friends who were musicians or who were interested in classical music, and as I was studying to become an architect, I found music to be very nurturing. Meeting Ernest Fleischmann some thirty years ago and working with him all these years since makes him my most important music teacher. He has introduced me to some of the most wonderful music and musicians I have ever heard and has helped me keep the flame alive.

Ernest also guided me through the early stages of my involvement in the Walt Disney Concert Hall project. We had worked together on the Hollywood Bowl for years, and by that point knew each other pretty well. When I was selected as the architect for the Concert Hall, the design parameters of the hall and the spirit of music that I drew upon—all of it came to me through Ernest. During the design process Ernest helped me gain access to all of the great musicians of the world who came to Los Angeles: Simon Rattle, Pierre Boulez, Kurt Sanderling, Zubin Mehta, and many others. Then, when Esa-Pekka Salonen officially joined the Los Angeles Philharmonic in 1992, he became another musical conduit for me. I listened to these musicians a lot. I asked them questions. I tried to understand how they think of space, how they approach playing in different spaces, how they accommodate themselves to a space, and what they think about when they perform. From those discussions I derived many of the principles that drove the aesthetics of the hall's design. Of course, from the very beginning the acousticians were also an important part of the process. I spent a lot of time with Minoru Nagata, and then with his protege, Yasuhisa Toyota, following Nagata's retirement.

Throughout the construction process, I was nervous about whether or not the Concert Hall really would be as great as we wanted it to be, as great as we hoped it would be. During the last few months of construction, when the floors were in but before the seats and stage were in, I couldn't wait to hear music in the hall. I remember feeling so nervous one night that I called Esa-Pekka, but he couldn't speak to me right away. His wife told me that he would call me back. While I waited for him to call I paced nervously around the room. When he called, I said, "Esa-Pekka, could you be free tomorrow afternoon at four o'clock to meet me at the Concert Hall?" And he said, "Of course I can do that." I then asked, "Would it be possible for you to bring an instrument?" The next day he met me at four and brought with him Martin Chalifour, the First Violinist of the Los Angeles Philharmonic. Martin had with him a backpack, a suitcase, and a violin case, and was wearing jeans, hiking boots, and a hard hat (hard hats were required to get into the hall). He opened up his bags, and lo and behold, took out a small recording device and some microphones to put around the hall. He then proceeded to take out his violin. As he put the bow to the violin, Esa-Pekka and I were watching from way up at the top of the hall. I grabbed Esa-Pekka's hand—the first notes were stunningly beautiful. They brought tears to my eyes and to Esa-Pekka's too. After a few minutes Esa-Pekka said, "This is the best sound I've ever heard in a hall." Even without seats and a stage, he knew it, and it did sound damn good.

The entire building was designed from the inside out and was meant to invite people to come inside. It was intended to be accessible to everyone, to feel casual, not pompous or overly formal, and I think those qualities, those goals, have been achieved. For me personally, the Concert Hall is a milestone. It has taken a long time to complete, and I have a lot of wounds from the process, but I also recognize that it is truly miraculous that the hall has been realized. As you look around the world and see other communities who try to do projects on this scale, and who often fail, you know how difficult and problematic such projects are and how thankful we should be that we were able to pull off this one.

There were so many people who made Walt Disney Concert Hall happen. But it never, ever could have turned out as well as it did without Ernest Fleischman, Esa-Pekka Salonen, Yasuhisa Toyota, Deborah Borda, and the musicians. And it never would have been built the way all of us intended it to be without the support of Diane Disney Miller. Diane's mother Lillian Disney started it all off with an enormous gift to Los Angeles, but in the end it was Diane and her husband Ron Miller who persevered with me through the darkest times. They were my partners; they made it happen, and we all owe them a great debt of gratitude.

All visitors must
check-in at office

AUTHORIZED PERSONNEL ONLY
HARDHATS · EYE PROTECTION
REQUIRED BEYOND THIS POINT

WARNING

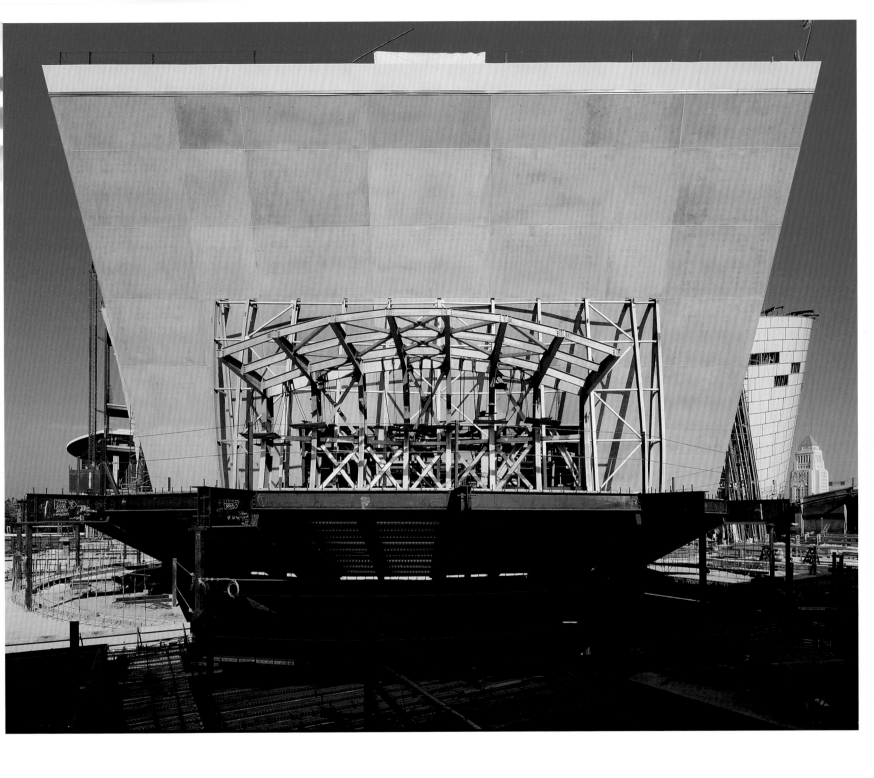

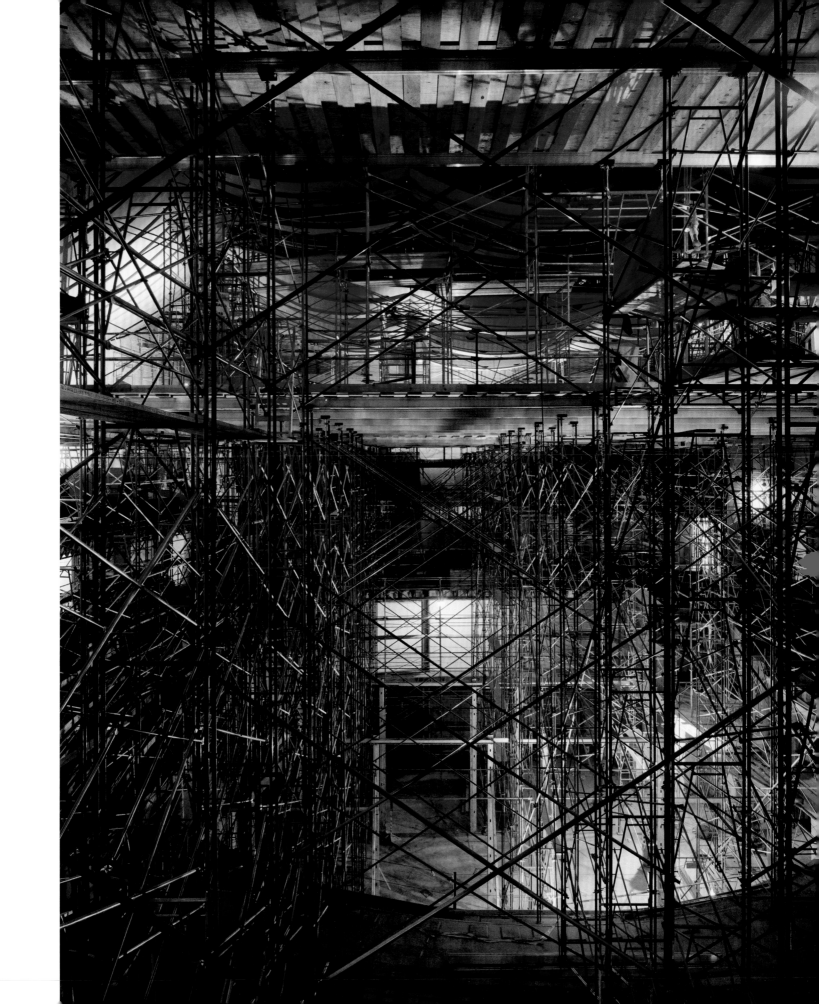

RICHARD WEINSTEIN:

Frank Gehry's talent is a unique, lyrical, plentiful, generous talent.
I think people like Frank come along once every one hundred years
who have that seemingly boundless ability to create and generate form.
You feel the joy of creation in the work itself. It may have a liberating
influence, but no one else will be able to do it nearly as well.

Richard Koshalek and Dana Hutt

The
Impossible
Becomes Possible:
The MAKING *of*
WALT DISNEY CONCERT HALL

Great works of architecture exude a sense of inevitability and fitness. Rooted and timeless, they appear as if they have always stood, the complications of their birth forgotten or briskly receding into the past. By definition, creating innovative public architecture—the most civic, costly, time-intensive, and physical of the arts— entails a certain amount of risk, strife, and negotiation. Potential hazards lie at every step of the process, from the planning and design stages to construction, occupancy, and critical reception. All buildings are realized through the confluence of many individuals who must work together to make them happen. But a building of ground-breaking design must also overcome the inherent apprehension of the multiple parties involved: the client, the bankers, the backers, the contractors, and the community. A large public commission that aspires to creative originality must also transcend forces beyond its immediate circumstance, obstacles of economics, politics, and leadership.

These challenges are worth the effort because a great cultural building provides a rare, memorable experience that contributes immeasurably to the identity of a city. The Eiffel Tower, the Sydney Opera House, and the Centre Pompidou are among the most celebrated examples of beloved civic icons that were highly controversial at the time of their creation. What is especially notable about the sixteen-year history of Walt Disney Concert Hall is its democratic process. Unlike François Mitterand's *grands projets* for cultural infrastructure and monuments in Paris in the 1980s, this building did not result from the patronage of the state, nor was it the product of a private commission. Walt Disney Concert Hall emerged—in fits and starts—from a collaboration of private individuals and civic, cultural, and corporate leadership in Los Angeles. The history of the Concert Hall is the story of a city's growing pains.

The roots of the Concert Hall's complicated public/private alliance can be traced to the inception of the Music Center. In 1955, the supervisors of the County of Los Angeles appointed Dorothy Buffum Chandler to chair a civic committee to promote the creation of a performing arts center for Los Angeles. The wife of *Los Angeles Times* publisher Norman Chandler and an imposing force herself, Buff Chandler secured County land on Bunker Hill and raised millions of dollars for the three-building complex designed by Welton Becket and completed in 1967.[1] She subsequently planned to establish a performing arts academy, and in 1968, her son-in-law F. Daniel Frost drafted an agreement between the Music Center and the County that reserved the County-owned Lot K for the conservatory.[2] The Music Center abandoned the plan, but retained a "slim legal hold" for expansion on the site.[3]

In the early 1980s, the Music Center considered, then scaled back, an ambitious plan to build three new theaters on Lot K. Music Center president Michael Newton recognized that the addition of a new hall for the Los Angeles Philharmonic would benefit the entire organization.[4] Meanwhile, the County supervisors were maneuvering to regain Lot K for more lucrative uses. They retained architect Barton Myers to develop plans to shift the site for the new concert hall to the Civic Center Mall, flanked by the County Courthouse and the Hall of Administration and across Grand Avenue from the Music Center, which would free Lot K for commercial development. In 1985, Myers presented these plans to Frost (then Music Center Chairman) and Lew Wasserman (former Music Center Foundation treasurer), who reacted with surprise and outrage, having expected to see plans for the Lot K site.[5] A stalemate ensued, which ended only when the County agreed to give the Music Center limited time to raise funds for the proposed building; otherwise, Lot K would revert back to the County.[6] A major donor soon stepped forward— to the shock of both the County and the Music Center.

THE GIFT

By all accounts, Lillian B. Disney's decision in May 1987 to bestow the Music Center with $50 million for a concert hall—"the largest single gift in the history of the United States for a cultural building"—was extraordinary.[7] An elegant, yet extremely modest woman, the eighty-seven-year-old widow of Walt Disney opted to stay in the background when the gift was announced. "Her wishes are to let the gift speak for itself," a spokesman said.[8] Since the mid-1950s, the Disney family had amassed millions of dollars from the licensing and sale of the commercial rights to the Walt Disney name.[9] The family had intended to start a charitable foundation, but urged by her daughter Diane Disney Miller to do something that would bring tangible results, Lillian Disney settled upon a concert hall to be named in honor

1 "History," Music Center Performing Arts Center of Los Angeles County, April 1, 2003, www.musiccenter.org/history.html.
2 Ted Vollmer, "Music Center Dispute Not Over Need to Expand—But Where?" *Los Angeles Times*, 22 February 1987.
3 F. Daniel Frost, interview by authors, Tucson, AZ, 15 December 2002.
4 Richard Weinstein, interview by authors, Santa Monica, CA, 26 November 2002; Joanne Kozberg, telephone conversation with authors, 21 January 2003.

5 Vollmer, "Music Center Dispute." Myers revised the plan in March 1987, in an effort to break the gridlock. He suggested shifting the new concert hall site to a bridge over Grand Avenue at the top of the Civic Mall (Leon Whiteson, "Harmony On The Hill With Disney Hall," *Los Angeles Times*, 29 April 1988).
6 Frost, interview.
7 Judith Michaelson, "Music Center Gift Keeps on Giving," *Los Angeles Times*, 16 May 1987.
8 Ibid.
9 Ronald E. Gother, interview by authors, Pasadena, CA, 15 October 2002.

RONALD GOTHER:

*Lillian Disney had a very positive
outlook on life. She was very kind and gentle
to everybody—just a very refined lady.*

COMPETITION MODEL FOR
WALT DISNEY CONCERT HALL
SHOWING LOT K SITE,
AS WELL AS LOTS Q AND W, 1988

LILLIAN DISNEY

DIANE DISNEY MILLER:

*It's strange that Walt Disney and Frank Gehry
never worked together; they might have. If Dad had lived
ten years longer, I know their paths would have crossed.*

of her late husband.[10] The Disney family had a long-standing relationship with the Music Center. Walt Disney, who had been friends with Buff Chandler, had participated in its initial stages. Lillian Disney was a founder of The Blue Ribbon, a volunteer group that supports the activities of the Music Center, and their daughters Miller and Sharon Lund were active on various boards.[11] The gift also reflected Walt Disney's love of music, as evident in his collaboration with the conductor Leopold Stokowski to combine classical music with animation in the 1940 film *Fantasia*, and his fascination with innovation and urban planning, as seen in the visionary plans for EPCOT (Experimental Prototype Community of Tomorrow).[12] A state-of-the-art concert hall in Downtown Los Angeles appeared to be the ideal memorial for Walt Disney and a powerful gift for Los Angeles.

Lillian Disney's two major conditions for the gift were that the hall be built on Lot K and that approval by the County of Los Angeles, the Music Center, and the Philharmonic Association be settled within thirty days. Other conditions included her approval of the architect, agreement from the County to build the parking garage, and a deadline to break ground by December 31, 1992—in five years—or the gift would be rescinded.[13] From the beginning, the County's hold on Lot K generated other conditions. Supervisor Edmund D. Edelman, although always supportive of the Music Center, insisted that commercial uses be included on the site so "as not to impede the county's revenue potential."[14] Mrs. Disney was amenable to the County's objectives, but stated "first and foremost, the concert hall...must be designed and built...to be one of the finest in the world and serve as a permanent tribute to my late husband, Walt Disney."[15] She requested that any adjoining development be designed by the same architect who designs the hall.[16]

Aside from Philharmonic leaders who greeted the news as "a dream come true," Mrs. Disney's gift was met with skepticism, even by critics at the *Los Angeles Times*. Dan Sullivan lamented the gift's purpose: "If only Mrs. Disney had offered the Music Center a $50-million gift, free and clear, to be used in whatever way would do its artists the most good!" Charles Champlin noted that the new hall would require operating monies and "possibly even supplementary capital funds that do not presently exist," concluding: "The irony of Mrs. Disney's offering is that it really is a challenge."[17]

THE CHAIRMANSHIP

Before the announcement was made, the Music Center leadership considered how best to organize the planning for Walt Disney Concert Hall. Frost recalls, "Mia [Frost, his then-wife] said the only person to do the work is Fred Nicholas."[18] An attorney, real estate developer, and "old hand at dealing with civic complexities," Frederick M. Nicholas had just spent six years overseeing the complicated design and construction process of Arata Isozaki's Grand Avenue building for The Museum of Contemporary Art, Los Angeles

10 Diane Disney Miller, interview by authors, San Francisco, CA, 25 October 2002.
11 Michaelson, "Music Center Gift."
12 Disney's drawings for EPCOT appeared in the MOCA-organized exhibition *At the End of the Century: One Hundred Years of Architecture* (1998).
13 Gother, interview.
14 Michaelson, "Music Center Gift."

15 Ted Vollmer, "For Disney Concert Hall; Take The $50-Million Gift, County Advised," *Los Angeles Times*, 12 June 1987.
16 Ibid.
17 Charles Champlin, "Disney's $50-Million Gift: Two Views; Hard Realities—and Challenges—of a Music Center Expansion," *Los Angeles Times*, 24 May 1987; Dan Sullivan, "Disney's $50-Million Gift: Two Views; Are We Creating Mausoleums Filled with Starving Artists?" *Los Angeles Times*, 24 May 1987.
18 Frost, interview.

(MOCA).[19] After making a few inquiries, Frost discovered that Nicholas enjoyed a reputation for an effective, no-nonsense management style, and immediately offered him the position of chair. Nicholas was stunned—he recently had been offered the chairmanship of MOCA, and now suddenly was confronted with another, equally challenging proposition—but agreed to talk with Lillian Disney. "I wanted to meet Mrs. Disney and to know whether she had a commitment to world-class architecture," Nicholas says. She told him that "world-class architecture was fine," and she wanted a garden and great acoustics.[20] Nicholas subsequently accepted the chairmanship for the Concert Hall, through which he felt he could continue his efforts to revitalize Downtown Los Angeles. He organized a committee to oversee the design and construction process— the Walt Disney Concert Hall Committee, which Frost dubbed "the Nicholas Committee"— with Nicholas, Disney family attorney Ron Gother, and Bob Wilson of the Disney Foundation as the original members.[21] He assembled a series of subcommittees for the selection of the architect, contractor, and construction manager (chaired by then-director of MOCA Richard Koshalek and developers Robert Maguire and James Thomas, respectively), with input from experts and the Music Center. He identified professionals in architecture, development, and acoustics to prepare the building program, and retained architectural historian Carol McMichael Reese to document the proceedings from the beginning. Above all, he wanted a process "clean and pure, free of extraneous political pressures."[22] Diane Disney Miller recalls, "It was a beautiful start."[23]

DEFINING THE PROGRAM

The mission was straightforward: to create a world-class concert hall with great acoustics. But what kind of concert hall would best suit the Los Angeles Philharmonic? How many seats were optimal? What type of connection between the orchestra and the audience was preferred? How would the building relate to the rest of the Music Center and to the greater urban context? To gain a clearer idea of the issues involved, Nicholas arranged a research tour of the great concert halls around the world. In November 1987, a small group, including Nicholas, Koshalek, Gother, Joanne C. Kozberg, Stanley Beyer, Royce Diener, Donna Vaccarino, Los Angeles Philharmonic executive director Ernest Fleischmann, cellist Barry Gold, and trombonist Byron Pebbles traveled to performances in major concert halls in Europe: Cologne, Berlin, Paris, Birmingham, Nottingham, London, Amsterdam, and The Hague.[24] In February 1988, a smaller group including Miller and her husband Ron visited concert halls in Tokyo and Osaka, Japan.[25] The Berlin Philharmonie, designed by Hans Scharoun, emerged as the group's favorite for its combination of acoustical excellence and audience intimacy.[26] Later, Fleischmann specifically cited the Berlin Philharmonie when he described what he wanted Walt Disney Concert Hall to be: a single-purpose hall that is inviting, open, and accessible to the street; a space that creates a close connection between the musicians and the surrounding audience; and a performance hall that has a rich, warm sound that preserves absolute clarity and transparency.[27]

19 Leon Whiteson, "Harmony on the Hill with Disney Hall," *Los Angeles Times*, 29 April 1988.
20 Frederick M. Nicholas, interview by authors, Playa del Rey, CA, 26 November 2002.
21 Frost, interview.
22 Whiteson, "Harmony on the Hill."
23 Miller, interview.

24 Kozberg, telephone conversation.
25 Ibid.
26 An article at the time also observed: "It seems to be generally agreed among musicians that, of all the large (2,000-plus-seat) concert halls built since World War II, only the wrap-around 1963 Berlin Philharmonic, designed by Hans Scharoun, manages to offer both really good sight lines and good acoustics" (Whiteson, "Harmony on the Hill").

Nicholas oversaw the building program, which was drafted by architect Donna Vaccarino and refined by Fleischmann. He also enlisted Charlotte Nassim, an architectural program consultant from Paris who had been recommended by the conductor Daniel Barenboim and Paris acoustical consultant Daniel Commins, who was teaching at the University of California, Los Angeles. Don Stastny, an architect based in Portland, Oregon, served as the professional advisor for the design commission.

Despite all these efforts, members of the Music Center's old guard still resisted the vision proposed for Walt Disney Concert Hall. Nicholas recalls that after a discussion about how the Concert Hall could become the focus for the city, much like the Sydney Opera House, one trustee told him and Koshalek not to go to any more trouble. "I'll tell you what to do," he said. "Get the drawings for the Dorothy Chandler Pavilion out of the drawing cabinet, hire the same architect, upgrade the mechanical, lighting and sound systems, and build the same damn building across the street."[28]

THE COMPETITION PROCESS

Nicholas considered the Architectural Subcommittee to be the most important of the subcommittees. To remove the possibility of politics, he avoided representatives from the City and County of Los Angeles, the Music Center, and the Los Angeles Philharmonic. Instead, he chose individuals who were involved with "culture and excitement and creativity" in the city: the directors of three art museums and deans from two architecture schools.[29] Accordingly, the five jurors were John Walsh from the J. Paul Getty Museum; Earl A. Powell from the Los Angeles County Museum of Art (LACMA); Richard Koshalek from MOCA, who chaired the subcommittee; Richard Weinstein from the University of California, Los Angeles; and Robert Harris from the University of Southern California. The charge of the subcommittee was to recommend an architect to the Walt Disney Concert Hall Committee, who would then make the final decision. In this way, the subcommittee members could "act on the basis of their conscience," and the Concert Hall Committee would be free to follow or disregard the subcommittee's recommendation.[30] According to the initial conditions of the gift, Mrs. Disney had the right to veto the selection and to choose the architect; however, she gave the Concert Hall Committee the authorization to make the decision.[31]

The competition preparation began in August 1987 with a list of eighty architects from around the world. To bring the list down to twenty-five architects, the subcommittee held numerous meetings in an open process, to which the Music Center leadership was invited. The twenty-five architects who were chosen then submitted their qualifications, and during a slide show at Mrs. Disney's house in Holmby Hills, the subcommittee reduced the field to six candidates: Goffried Böhm of Cologne; Harry Cobb of New York; Frank Gehry of Venice, California; Hans Hollein of Vienna; Renzo Piano of Genoa; and James Stirling of London. The jurors looked

27 Ernest Fleischmann, "The Design and Building Process" (paper presented at the Walt Disney Concert Hall symposium, The Getty Center, 20 April 2002); Ernest Fleischmann, interview by authors, Hollywood, CA, 17 December 2002.
28 Nicholas, interview; Richard Koshalek, "The Design and Building Process" (paper presented at the Walt Disney Concert Hall symposium, The Getty Center, 20 April 2002).

29 Nicholas, interview.
30 Weinstein, interview.
31 Leon Whiteson, "Four Different Visions of Disney Concert Hall," *Los Angeles Times*, 8 December 1988; Nicholas, interview.

for diversity among the architects to make the choice easier and to get the unusually talented into the mix. The subcommittee conducted interviews with the six architects, and then, as previously agreed upon, the subcommittee and committee could each eliminate one candidate for any reason. At this time, two architects were dropped.

THE FINAL FOUR

On March 17, 1988, Nicholas and Koshalek announced the four finalists: Goffried Böhm, Frank Gehry, Hans Hollein, and James Stirling. All but Gehry were winners of the Pritzker Architecture Prize, architecture's highest honor. Böhm, best known for the Church of the Pilgrimage in Neviges, Germany, received the Pritzker in 1986. Hollein—the winner of the 1985 prize—was the architect of two acclaimed modern art museums in Mönchengladbach and Frankfurt, Germany. Stirling, who won the Pritzker in 1981, had designed (with partner Michael Wilford) a number of cultural buildings, including the Neue Staatsgalerie and the Chamber Theatre in Stuttgart, the Clore Gallery at the Tate Museum in London, and the Arthur H. Sackler Museum at Harvard University. Gehry, the only local architect on the list, had built work throughout Los Angeles, including the Aerospace Museum, MOCA's Temporary Contemporary, and the Goldwyn Library in Hollywood. "In making the decision," Nicholas said, "the subcommittee applied what they called a 'ripeness test,' to determine whether the architect was at that stage in his career that he could be producing his greatest work."[32] Each architect received $75,000 to prepare the competition materials.

As soon as the final four were announced, members of the subcommittee started "getting flack" from the Music Center and others close to the project: "You can't pick Frank Gehry; we're going to be the laughingstock of the whole universe."[33] Gehry's popular reputation as an architectural "wild man" for his use of unconventional materials, for a rawness that exposes process (like the work of his Venice artist friends), and for an idiosyncratic, personal form-making that evokes the disunity and energy of vernacular Los Angeles clearly scared the elites of Downtown Los Angeles. Ironically, his work also demonstrated a highly pragmatic business sense. By this time Gehry was internationally recognized as one of the most progressive architects in the country. His work had been included (although he agreed to it reluctantly) in the Museum of Modern Art's *Deconstructivist Architecture* exhibition in 1988. At the very moment he was named as a finalist in the Concert Hall competition, down the street, MOCA was presenting a major retrospective of his work organized by the Walker Art Center in Minneapolis. Moreover, Gehry had previously collaborated with the Los Angeles Philharmonic on the renovation of the Hollywood Bowl in phases from 1970 to 1982. He also had two other music venues to his credit: the Merriweather Post Pavilion in Columbia, Maryland, and the Concert Pavilion near San Francisco. When asked about the experience of each of the finalists, Fleischmann mentioned Gehry's music pavilions, stating, "We [the Philharmonic] performed there [in Concord] with Leonard Bernstein and found it terrific to play in."[34] One might presume that Gehry was the shoo-in candidate and that the competition was partisan, but this was not the case. "It was really the

32 Judith Michaelson, "Finalists Pared to 4 in Competition for Disney Hall," *Los Angeles Times*, 18 March 1988.

33 Nicholas, interview with authors, 26 November 2002.

absolute opposite," says Fleischmann. "It was loaded against Frank with that Music Center lot; you know what the feeling was about Frank in the city."[35] Among themselves, the subcommittee took a straw vote after selecting the final four, and the winner was Stirling. He was a prominent European architect of the moment and his designs were not considered extreme, while Hollein was seen as perhaps too quirky.[36]

Each of the finalists received a highly detailed, itemized program for the design commission in three booklets—what became known as the "play book." The competition's three main foci were summarized as challenges and opportunities.[37] The first challenge was to create a "conceptual link" to the Music Center. The second was "to develop the site and building to its optimum potential as a focal point in Downtown Los Angeles." Highlighting the site's role as an urban link, the program cited the opportunity to design a civic plaza "reflecting the warmth and friendliness of Southern California." In addition to the design of the concert hall, the architects were also asked to do a preliminary planning analysis for Lots Q and W2, to the east of Lot K. That program comprised commercial and retail space on the ground floor and offices above. The third challenge related to the acoustics of the hall, which, the play book stipulated, "should produce good natural sound: strong, clear, and direct sound without distortions." The architects were encouraged to design to acoustical parameters. Above all, the program stated, "the concept must represent an inspired solution, one that honors the creativity and integrity of Walt Disney and upholds the standard of artistic excellence of the Music Center's resident companies."[38]

In July, the four finalists returned to Los Angeles for a competition briefing, followed by a kick-off reception at Lillian Disney's house. The event revealed an aspect of the donor that would prove crucial later in the competition. Weinstein recalls: "There were flowers everywhere at the house, including an explosion of [blooms] along the border of the lawn where the party was held. It was clear that Mrs. Disney was an inveterate and passionate gardener. The evening was filled with ceremony, speeches, champagne, and lots of people, and architects cruised around like sharks."[39]

FINAL SELECTION

After the briefing, the architects met with the subcommittee two more times: for a concept review in September and for the final presentations in late November. The two-stage look at the design development allowed the subcommittee to assess not only the progress of each design concept, but more important, how well the architects listened and responded to feedback from the earlier review. As Nicholas had said earlier in the process, they were not looking for a final design "so much as a way to judge the architect's ability to solve problems and work with the client group."[40]

In early November, as the final presentations approached, a member of the Walt Disney Concert Hall Committee grew increasingly concerned about the possibility of Gehry being selected. This committee member strongly proposed that the Architectural Subcommittee provide

34 Judith Michaelson, "6 Architects Are Candidates for Disney Hall," *Los Angeles Times*, 15 January 1988.
35 Fleischmann, interview.
36 Weinstein, interview. Stirling had also been one of the three finalists in the architecture selection process for the Getty Center.

37 *Architecture program for the Walt Disney Concert Hall Design Commission, volume 1* (Los Angeles: The Music Center of Los Angeles County, 1988), 5.
38 Ibid., 26.
39 Weinstein, interview.

THE HOLLYWOOD BOWL,
RENOVATION WITH
ACOUSTICAL SPHERES DESIGNED
BY FRANK GEHRY, 1980

RICHARD WEINSTEIN:

I was concerned about a mission statement....
I wanted to see how carefully the architects would
listen. It's one thing to get a program and make
sure you've got every space on the program in
the building. It's much harder to catch the spirit
of what the client wants and to have your design be
responsive to those intangible messages.

JOHN WALSH:

I will say that we could be thought of as a pretty closed little circle of
partisans for advanced contemporary architecture.... So if I were a businessman,
a banker, or a reluctant trustee of the Philharmonic...I might well
look at this five and say, well, yeah, of course they're going to come up with...
an architect who's going to cost us a fortune and for uncertain results.
What I think they weren't accepting, couldn't see, didn't know about, was the
fact that Frank had proven himself so thoroughly as a guy who could deliver
a building on time, on budget.

commentary only and not final ranking as part of their recommendation. Furthermore, he demanded, they were not to speak with the press. The subcommittee resisted. All of the members decided to quit together if they were prevented from providing the committee with an uncensored recommendation, and at the subcommittee's suggestion, Walsh drafted a resignation letter. The subcommittee's decision to engage in a public dialogue diminished the conflict and the crisis was averted. At the end of November, each of the architects presented their submissions—a narrative, eight panels of drawings, a site model, and a Lot K model—to the Concert Hall Committee and Architectural Subcommittee.

After careful deliberation and a difference of opinion expressed by one subcommittee member, the final decision of the subcommittee became unanimous. On December 5, the Disney Concert Hall Committee gathered in the former Crocker Bank Center on Hope Street to hear the subcommittee's recommendation. Lillian Disney wore her lucky red dress.[41] Each of the five subcommittee members made a presentation to the group, explaining his reasons for the selection. Because of Weinstein's passionate commitment to the most innovative architecture, he began the discussion; Walsh was given the closing position due to his calm, confident manner and his clear understanding of the decision-making process and the uncertainties involved.

The subcommittee provided a ranking of the four architects, and at the bottom was Gottfried Böhm. In Böhm's scheme, a massive dome superstructure of reinforced concrete creates a grand atrium that contains all the functional spaces. The concert hall is raised off the ground. Surrounding the dome are buildings topped by roof gardens, stair and lift towers, escalators, and bridges. Walsh considered Böhm's idea fabulous and impossible, with a German idealism and "romanticism in these vast interior spaces with zillions of tiny people."[42] Weinstein called it preposterous: "I found Böhm's sort of romantic, Wagnerian excess to be really a way of showing contempt for Los Angeles and the whole enterprise."[43] The *Los Angeles Times* likened it to "a huge Brunnhilde bra cup in an Olympian-scale performance of the *Twilight of the Gods*."[44]

The project by Stirling also disappointed. Relating the design to the tradition of monumental public buildings and the "populist aspect" of contemporary places of culture and entertainment, Stirling created an ensemble of abstract geometrical forms unified at ground level by a grand concourse.[45] Like Böhm, Stirling's design lifted most of the primary spaces off the ground—which some members of the subcommittee considered an elitist gesture.[46] In the design, a square box office that is topped by a rotating electronic billboard is situated at the corner of Grand and First streets. The cylindrical concert hall, dubbed "Snowflake" for its tiered, interlocking balconies, places the conductor and orchestra almost centrally in the room. According to the competition consultants, the hall's circular shape had low probability of attaining an outstanding acoustical environment.[47] During the concept review, Stirling was asked to redesign the balcony in order to improve sight lines, but returned in November with no change in the design. "I was disturbed by his kind of belligerence," Weinstein says.[48] In addition, as Walsh pointed out, the project could be anywhere, Detroit or Düsseldorf.[49]

40 Whiteson, "Harmony on the Hill."
41 Gother, interview.
42 John Walsh, Walt Disney Concert Hall Committee Report of the Architectural Subcommittee, 5 December 1988.
43 Weinstein, interview.
44 Whiteson, "Four Different Visions."

45 James Stirling and Michael Wilford, narrative, Walt Disney Concert Hall design commission, 1988.
46 Weinstein, interview.
47 Fred Stegeman and Fritz W. Kastner, memorandum, Walt Disney Concert Hall: Review of the Four Design Architect Submissions, 30 November 1988.

PRESENTATIONS, top left to right:
HANS HOLLEIN, JAMES STIRLING,
GOTTFRIEND BÖHM. left: FRANK GEHRY,
right: THE ARCHITECTURAL SUBCOMMITTEE
AT THE FINAL PRESENTATIONS
(from left: RICHARD WEINSTEIN, JOHN WALSH,
EARL A. POWELL, ROBERT HARRIS,
AND RICHARD KOSHALEK)

FREDRICK M. NICHOLAS:
It took a number of years to get organized, to get all of the work done, and to hire the architect, because this was a very, very political process, and I wanted to keep the process from exploding. It was an incredible process…because we had participation from all the experts.

The jazzy improvisation of Hollein's final design appealed to some subcommittee members, but ultimately misfired. His improvisation as well as "appetite" was much in evidence during the competition.[50] During a jumbled concept review, Hollein displayed four alternative schemes, and for the final presentation, he sent a second, alternative model, which was prohibited by the rules. Intended to be "light, exuberant, joyful with a touch of distinction and splendor," the postmodern scheme comprises a large horizontal monolith broken up by an assemblage of varied forms, colors, and materials—white marble, green quartzite, red sandstone, gray and green granite, and aluminum.[51] Within the building are literal allusions to Walt Disney, including "a Walt Disney sculpture listening to the concert from a high pedestal" and a "Mickey Mouse bridge."[52] The design aims to connect to a populist cultural context by anticipating a future Academy Awards ceremony, with Oscar in the form of caryatids reminiscent of the Vienna-Musikverein,"[53] which Weinstein termed "beyond tasteless."[54] Furthermore, consultants deemed its uneven hexagonal concert hall to be acoustically flawed.[55] The design's relation to the urban context is also problematic. "The project is a long way from Los Angeles in being so enclosed and compacted, so turned inward, and the relation to the Music Center is very tenuous," Walsh reported.[56] Hollein placed a "slow second" in the competition.[57]

Gehry won the commission decisively, with a thoroughly considered design and the potential for a highly original architectural statement. With its generosity of openness and space and a lush garden, Gehry's scheme evidenced a full understanding of what a building in Los Angeles should be. Its great glass-roofed conservatory, terraces, and facade were accessible to culturally and economically diverse audiences—as a "living room" for the city.[58] In response to the acoustical and social requirements for the new concert hall, Gehry created a more visceral and immediate experience through a surround stage.[59] Unlike those of his competitors, Gehry's design also takes into account how musicians will experience the building and includes many special features, such as the musician's garden. The design responds both to Fleischmann's concerns and to Mrs. Disney's love of gardens and flowers. The narrative submitted by Gehry capitalized on botanical metaphors, depicting the concert hall as a "garden oasis" in the city, which would grow out of the plaza in a "floral form of French limestone."[60] From the cost and project management consultants' reports it was clear that Gehry was the only one of the four architects who had absorbed the program and had truly listened.[61]

Now that Gehry was the clear winner, one question remained. How could the Architectural Subcommittee make the Concert Hall Committee comfortable with the selection? At the December 5 presentation, they let the diplomatic Getty director John Walsh close the case for Gehry:

48 Weinstein, interview.
49 Walsh, Report of the Architectural Subcommittee.
50 Weinstein, interview.
51 Hans Hollein, narrative, Walt Disney Concert Hall design commission, 1988.
52 Ibid.
53 Ibid.
54 Weinstein, interview.
55 Stegeman and Kastner, memorandum.

56 Walsh, Report of the Architectural Subcommittee.
57 Ibid.
58 Leon Whiteson, "Frank Gehry 'Always Wanted to Work Big,'" Los Angeles Times, 18 December 1988.
59 Michael Maltzan, interview by authors, Pasadena, CA, 26 October 2002.
60 Frank Gehry, narrative, Walt Disney Concert Hall design commission, 1988.
61 Stegeman and Kastner, memorandum; Weinstein, interview.

MODEL OF FRANK GEHRY'S
COMPETITION-WINNING
DESIGN FOR WALT DISNEY
CONCERT HALL, 1988

MICHAEL MALTZAN:

*I remember leaving that meeting and…walking down
past the site and thinking…I was about the luckiest architect
I could possibly imagine on the planet… because we were
doing a project and were actually producing something that
was living up to the aspirations of the city.*

from left: FRANK GEHRY
WITH HIS COMPETITION-WINNING
MODEL AND DIANE DISNEY MILLER,
FRED NICHOLAS, AND ERNEST
FLEISCHMANN, 1988

For me, Gehry wins this competition hands down, by a wide margin. This is both for the qualities he's shown in his career, and for his entry, which seems to be much the best, and frankly the only one I'd really want to see built for the Philharmonic.

Because some of you are still uneasy at the idea of Gehry on this job, I just want to say something about why I think he's such a logical choice—in fact the safest choice on the list.

Gehry's popular reputation is a funny thing, and he's partly to blame. For you, like a lot of people, his trademark may be chain link and plywood, cheap materials and a kind of bohemian thumb-your-nose attitude. And you may think of him as on the fringe artistically. Actually his biggest clients see him quite differently. Gehry takes a lot of pride in being a reliable, down-to-earth, businesslike builder of buildings that work. Don't forget that he started with shopping centers and malls and commercial developments—Santa Monica Place is just one—and he's done building after building on time, on budget.[62]

"We waited five, six days and gradually [the Concert Hall Committee] came around," says Nicholas, as the subcommittee was able to explain its reasons for selecting Gehry.[63] Once the subcommittee had given their recommendation, the leadership of the Music Center and Architectural Subcommittee made a persuasive case for Gehry. They reminded the press and the Concert Hall Committee that you choose an architect, not a design. Furthermore, it was reasoned that the architect should be a problem-solver and someone responsive to the context of Los Angeles. The Music Center leadership involved in the process (Frost, Kozberg, Franklin Murphy, and others) as well as Nicholas met with individual members of the Disney family and the Concert Hall Committee to encourage them to accept the Architectural Subcommittee's decision. Gehry's selection was announced on December 12, 1988.

Reaction to the selection was swift and largely positive. Leon Whiteson, architecture critic for the *Los Angeles Times*, called the design "quintessentially Angeleno" and chronicled the rise of Gehry's star.[64] Gehry himself described the event as "more than a little miraculous."[65] An editorial in the *Los Angeles Times* praised his plan for the Concert Hall as "marvelous, a brilliant and innovative addition to the Music Center" and stated "it is not surprising that his plan was the unanimous choice."[66] The good times continued for Gehry; a few months after receiving the Walt Disney Concert Hall commission, he was named the 1989 recipient of the Pritzker Architecture Prize. Ada Louise Huxtable, a member of the Pritzker jury, cited Gehry's gifts as an innovator: "He takes chances; he works close to the edge; he pushes boundaries beyond previous limits. There are times when he misses the mark, and times when the breakthrough achieved alters everyone else's vision as well. And he believes, as most architects do, that it is always the next project that will realize his aims."[67] Walt Disney Concert Hall was poised to be that next project.

62 Walsh, Report of the Architectural Subcommittee.
63 Nicholas, interview.
64 Leon Whiteson, "Gehry's Disney Hall Design 'Quintessentially Angeleno,'" *Los Angeles Times*, 13 December 1988.

65 Whiteson, "Frank Gehry 'Always Wanted to Work Big.'"
66 Editorial, "Creativity at Work," *Los Angeles Times*, 14 December 1988.
67 The Pritzker Architecture Prize, 1 April 2003, www.pritzkerprize.com.

Gehry's competition-winning project for Walt Disney Concert Hall marked the beginning of the design process. Now, with the architect named, the client group could begin to better address the complex set of issues involved in the Concert Hall's planning and implementation. Among the key concerns were the acoustics of the hall, use of the overall site, urban planning beyond the immediate site, and the contractual agreements among the entities involved.

The most straightforward and critical factor influencing the design of the Concert Hall was the choice of the acoustician. During the architectural competition, it was understood that the subcommittee was recommending the architect, not the project, as the design of the project would likely undergo considerable change once an expert acoustician (to be selected in part by the architect) and the orchestra's music director became truly collaborative partners in the hall's design. A good working relationship between architect and acoustician was crucial. During the research tour to Japan, the Walt Disney Concert Hall Committee was most impressed by the bright, clear, yet warm sound of Tokyo's acclaimed Suntory Hall, which had been built in 1986. The acoustician of that hall was Dr. Minoru Nagata, a pioneer of architectural acoustics who had designed more than sixty halls and theaters during a forty-year career.[68] In December 1988, Gehry flew to Tokyo to meet Nagata, who commented on their instant rapport: "I liked Mr. Gehry immediately for his frankness."[69] For his first major project overseas, Nagata and his assistant, Yasuhisa Toyota (who became chief concert-hall acoustician upon Nagata's retirement in 1994), traveled to Los Angeles monthly and worked with Gehry by fax machine. Gehry's office started the design for the Concert Hall from scratch and made eighty-two models at one-sixteenth-inch scale, with four concert-hall prototypes: Berlin, Vienna, Amsterdam, and Boston. Gehry, Fleischmann, and Nagata chose the workable models, none of which had balconies, elite seats, or boxes.[70] The design of the hall and the acoustics evolved together.

At the same time, Gehry began to redesign the entire project, which led to a more troublesome matter: Who was the client? The Los Angeles Philharmonic—the resident company of the Concert Hall—was but one of the various constituencies that made up the multi-headed client, which also comprised the County of Los Angeles, the Music Center, the Disney family, and the Walt Disney Concert Hall Committee, all of which were pulling in multiple directions. Nicholas continued to serve as the project's "glue," joining the boards of both the Los Angeles Philharmonic and the Music Center. He also met daily with the project manager Fred Stegeman, weekly with the County's lawyers, and regularly with Mrs. Disney.

With multiple constituencies, the governance of the project became very complicated, and the decision-making, cumbersome and lengthy.[71] Furthermore, each group had its own ideas about the project. The Los Angeles Philharmonic wanted to relocate its offices there. The County's objectives were more problematic and contributed to various program changes—and delays. Despite the strong support of Supervisors Edelman, Kenneth Hahn, and Deane Dana, the county

68 Nobuko Hara, "Acoustician Sounding Out New Ideas for Disney Hall," *Los Angeles Times*, 13 October 1989.
69 Ibid.
70 Craig Webb, interview by authors, Santa Monica, CA, 13 December 2002.

71 Kozberg, telephone conversation; Larry Gordon and Diane Haithman, "Early Start on Disney Hall Project Was Calculated Risk," *Los Angeles Times*, 27 August 1994.

sought to protect taxpayers, and insisted upon an income-generating use of the public land. A chamber music hall, included in the original program, was replaced by a 350-room Ritz-Carlton Hotel, which was also designed by Gehry. The addition of the hotel to the site led to further changes in the site plan, the Concert Hall design, and the size of the parking garage, all of which increased project costs and delays. A labor dispute between the Community Redevelopment Agency of Los Angeles (CRA) and the hotel developer later terminated the deal, and the hotel was off the boards.[72] Gehry's office designed, redesigned, and then redesigned the project again.

Significantly, the commission for Walt Disney Concert Hall arrived in the Gehry office at a transitional moment. A year after the award, the office began to transform itself into a global operation, growing from a staff of thirty to seventy-five and implementing new computer applications.[73] In 1989, the office typically worked with executive architects on major projects— a problematic relationship, as executive architects can be indifferent to design and are often inclined to commit their best resources to their own projects. For the Concert Hall, Gehry chose the firm of Dworsky Associates. But the competition-winning design that Dworsky agreed to oversee was to evolve radically into one of unprecedented complexity. In 1991, led by Gehry's partner Jim Glymph, the Gehry office began to use CATIA (Computer-Aided Three-dimensional Interactive Application), a computer program that originally had been developed for the French aerospace industry to translate complex three-dimensional objects into construction documents. Dworsky Associates had difficulty using and trusting the software and were cautious legally and architecturally.[74] The resulting working drawings were poorly organized, confusing, and unfinished.[75] Only during the bidding for the project were the drawings found to be virtually useless, and contractors sought to protect themselves with exorbitantly high bids.

THE COMPLEXITY OF PRODUCING AMBITIOUS ARCHITECTURE

A complex mesh of political, planning, management, and bidding problems led to the construction shutdown of Walt Disney Concert Hall in November 1994. Insiders cited delays caused by the complicated negotiations with the County and numerous redesigns related to acoustics. Others pointed to the difficult nature of the decision-making process, which had come to include Dworsky Associates, a construction consortium of three companies, an acoustics firm, other management and consulting entities, as well as music director Esa-Pekka Salonen.[76] The project had been fast-tracked—a common, if sometimes risky, strategy in which construction is begun before detailed drawings and a maximum building cost are finalized—so that ninety-two-year-old Lillian Disney could see progress. The official groundbreaking had taken place on December 10, 1992—just days before the five-year deadline for the start of construction, a condition that had accompanied Lillian Disney's founding gift. The project had braved civil unrest, a major earthquake, and a recession that struck Los Angeles in the early 1990s. The 1994 Northridge earthquake caused the structure of the Concert

72 Nicholas, interview; Kozberg, telephone conversation; Barbara Isenberg, "Disney Hall Background," Los Angeles Times, 7 April 1991.
73 Joseph Giovannini, "Scissors, Papers, Stone: Frank Gehry and the Making of the Disney Concert Hall," *Los Angeles Times Magazine*, 22 November 1992; Maltzan, interview; Webb, interview.

74 Webb, interview with authors, 13 December 2002.
75 Joseph Giovannini, "Disney Hall and Gehry in Deal," New York Times, 7 August 1997; Maltzan, interview.
76 Gordon and Haithman, "Early Start Was Calculated Risk."

RONALD GOTHER:

The county envisioned us, the Disney family entities,
as if we were a developer and assumed that we were developing
for our own private benefit a building on county land.
They never could understand that this was their building....
And so they imposed restriction after restriction.

ROBERT B. EGELSTON:

What I kept in mind were two things: Great cities do
great things, and this is a great city. I cannot imagine
this project failing. I suppose I said that a thousand times:
Great cities do great things, and this project cannot fail.

from left: COUNTY SUPERVISOR
DEANE DANA, COUNTY SUPERVISOR
GLORIA MOLINA, SHARON LUND,
ERNEST FLEISCHMANN,
FRED NICHOLAS, JAMES THOMAS,
FRANK GEHRY, EDMUND EDELMAN,
DIANE DISNEY MILLER AT THE
GROUND-BREAKING CEREMONY
FOR WALT DISNEY CONCERT HALL,
DECEMBER 10, 1992

Hall to be changed to a steel-brace frame, which further increased costs since eighty percent of the steel was already purchased.[77] Costs for construction and materials and for professional and consulting fees continued to escalate.

In August 1994, the project reached a new nadir, raising fresh doubts about its future, when Walt Disney Concert Hall officials announced that the hall, estimated at $210 million in 1992, would now cost an additional $50 million.[78] In response, Richard S. Volpert, an attorney for the County, stated that the County was not committed to the complex and costly design: "If you throw enough money at it, you can build an atom bomb, fly to the moon, build the [Walt] Disney Concert Hall."[79] Four months later, County officials threatened to declare the project in default of its lease agreement and called for making the County-owned parking garage a stand-alone structure.[80] The Music Center leadership, now under Chairman Robert B. Egelston, quietly regrouped. They brought in a Houston-based management company, Hines Interest, to reassess cost estimates. They also appointed Harry Hufford, a former Music Center acting president and County chief administrator, as a new full-time volunteer chief executive officer to oversee Hines and fund-raising.[81] But still the project lay dormant, with obstacles so great its recovery appeared nearly impossible. By 1996, despite an array of international commissions including a new Guggenheim Museum under construction in Spain, Gehry said the floundering Walt Disney Concert Hall project made him feel like a pariah in Los Angeles.[82]

CHANGE OF MOMENTUM

With its construction on hold for nearly two years, Walt Disney Concert Hall began to show signs of life in 1996 through press articles and other key events that sent emergency signals to Los Angeles's civic leadership. Newspaper reportage and editorials were vital to the advocacy of the Concert Hall throughout its long gestation and particularly during the prolonged delays.[83] In November 1992, architect and writer Joseph Giovannini helped to counter superficial criticism of the Concert Hall's exterior by explaining Gehry's design process and the underlying principles behind its unusual forms in the *Los Angeles Times Magazine*.[84] The next month, Herbert Muschamp, architecture critic for the *New York Times*, praised the project to a national audience as a "magic democracy": "For once, an architectural imagination soars to the level of the highest civic hopes."[85] In October 1996, Nicholai Ouroussoff, the newly appointed architecture critic for the *Los Angeles Times*, wrote a front-page article heightening attention to the hall's increasingly precarious status.[86] Each of these articles—especially Ouroussoff's challenging piece—not only raised public awareness about the Concert Hall and its architecture, but more important, heartened members of the Disney family who were very discouraged by this time.

77 Webb, interview.
78 Gordon and Haithman, "Early Start Was Calculated Risk."
79 Ibid.
80 Diane Haithman and Carla Rivera, "Disney Hall Site in Danger of Lease Default, County Warns," *Los Angeles Times*, 21 December 1994.
81 Diane Haithman, "Unfinished Symphony? The Dream of a 'World-Class' Music Facility Is Entangled in So Many Financial Problems that Its Future May Be in Jeopardy," *Los Angeles Times*, 27 February 1995.
82 Larry Gordon, "Gehry Tries to Rebuild Image After Disney Hall," *Los Angeles Times*, 30 May 1996.

83 Among the particularly persuasive editorials that appeared in the *Los Angeles Times* were commentaries by Frederick M. Nicholas ("In the Spirit of Our Times," December 21, 1992), Richard Weinstein ("Great Cities, Great Public Works," August 30 1994; "A Different Kind of 'City on a Hill,'" June 12, 1996), Esa-Pekka Salonen ("Beyond the Building, February 1, 1995), and Michael Webb ("A Grand Public Building for a City Sadly Lacking," April 16 1995).
84 Giovannini, "Scissors, Papers, Stone."
85 Herbert Muschamp, "Gehry's Disney Hall: A Matterhorn for Music," *New York Times*, 13 December 1992.
86 Nicolai Ouroussoff, "MOCA Becomes Advocate for Disney Hall Construction," *Los Angeles Times*, 7 October 1996.

From a different perspective, *Los Angeles Times* music critic Mark Swed alerted the Los Angeles music community to the benefit Walt Disney Concert Hall would bring to the Los Angeles Philharmonic. In two articles, also published in early October 1996, Swed described how the Philharmonic had enchanted audiences in Paris during their three-week residency at the Stravinsky festival that fall. At Théâtre du Châtelet, the orchestra played in the same room as the audience, just as it would in the proscenium-less Walt Disney Concert Hall. He wrote:

> [I]t is notable that the voice [the Philharmonic] did finally find was a voice the hometown crowd at the Dorothy Chandler Pavilion never hears. In the live, intimate acoustic of the [Théâtre du] Châtelet, the Philharmonic sound has an arresting immediacy…. And the word around Paris, at the moment, is that if more Angelenos could hear sound like this, they would be just as ecstatic as the Parisians were Tuesday, and there would be no stopping the building of the new [Walt] Disney Concert Hall.[87]

In a subsequent article, Swed argued that the opportunity to hear the Philharmonic in a superior, vivid acoustical setting was a reason "to lobby hard" for the Concert Hall: "Players, patrons and management are sounding newly optimistic about the troubled hall, for which $150 million must be raised (a third of that by June 1). With this residency, one Philharmonic supporter announced, ice cream bar in hand during an intermission, everything is changed."[88] Fleischmann believes that the residency at the Théâtre du Châtelet marked a turning point in the fund-raising campaign and in the attitude of Los Angeles towards the Concert Hall, by showing the absolute necessity of a hall that would match the artistry of the Philharmonic.[89]

Directly on the heels of this media push came the first Los Angeles exhibition of the design materials for Walt Disney Concert Hall, which were shown on MOCA's plaza from October 27, 1996, to April 27, 1997. MOCA director Koshalek organized the exhibition *Walt Disney Concert Hall: A Celebration of Music and Architecture* as a blatant act of cultural advocacy and public education. Presented free and open to the public around the clock, the exhibition comprised Gehry's large-scale models, computer renderings, a large collection of working models, a full-scale mock-up of a limestone wall, and a specially designed pavilion containing a huge model of the Concert Hall's interior. Some of the work had previously been on view at the 1991 Venice Biennale, where it had captivated international audiences.[90] The Los Angeles presentation was an intentionally "aggressive move to help rescue the financially embattled" Concert Hall.[91] Fund-raising was critical to meet a new deadline set by the County to raise at least $50 million of a $150 million shortfall by June 1997.[92]

In an exceedingly rare display of professional support, the international architecture community also rallied behind the yet-unbuilt work. "Build It and They Will Come" read the headline of a full-page advertisement for Walt Disney Concert Hall in the front section of the *Los Angeles Times* on March 4, 1997. A long list of architects—local, national, and international—followed, as well as the names of curators, editors, publishers, critics, and designers who

87 Mark Swed, "The 'Rite' Springs to Life Under Salonen's Baton," *Los Angeles Times*, 3 October 1996.
88 Mark Swed, "Philharmonic Making No Mistakes as Tourist," *Los Angeles Times*, 8 October 1996.
89 Fleischmann, interview.

90 Giovannini, "Scissors, Papers, Stone."
91 Ouroussoff, "MOCA Advocate for Disney Hall"; Diane Haithman, "Disney Hall Seeks Funds as Deadlines Draw Closer," *Los Angeles Times*, 26 December 1996.
92 Ouroussoff, "MOCA Advocate for Disney Hall."

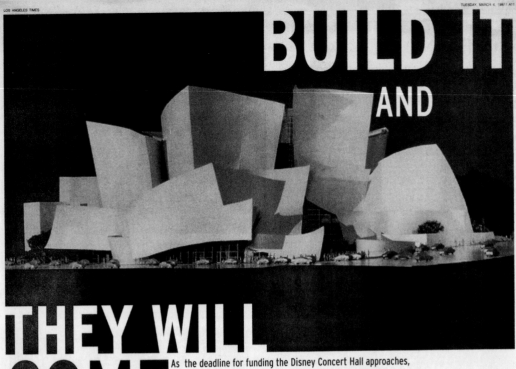

BUILD IT AND THEY WILL COME

As the deadline for funding the Disney Concert Hall approaches, the architects and designers of Los Angeles, and their colleagues in the U.S. and abroad, wish to offer their support for this visionary design by Frank Gehry and to recognize the generosity of the gift made by the Disney family.

All of us who love music and the arts and who care about the place of our city in the next millennium understand the central importance of this building and the role it will play in the cultural life of our community.

Raimond Abraham, New York
Trevor Abramson Architects, Santa Monica
William Adams, FAIA, Santa Monica
Ralph Allen, FFAIA, Santa Ana
Ronald A. Altoon, FAIA, Los Angeles
Emilio Ambasz, New York
Anthony Ames, Atlanta
Tadao Ando, Osaka
Paola Antonelli, New York
Kiyokazu Arai, Tokyo
Wiel Arets, Maastricht
Joseph A. Balbona, Los Angeles
Verr Bateman & Derek Soltes, Los Angeles
Barbara Bestor, AIA, Los Angeles
Aaron Betsky, San Francisco
Robert N. Blair, Santa Monica
Julia Bloomfield, Santa Monica
Lance Bird, AIA, Pasadena
Biro + De Jarnett, Venice
Tom Blurock, Costa Mesa
Cheryl Brantner, Los Angeles
Will Bruder, Phoenix
Michael Burch, Los Angeles
Burning Box, Los Angeles
Ben Caffey, Los Angeles
Israel Callas Shortridge Associates, Inc., Beverly Hills
La Canada Design Group, Pasadena
Victoria Casasco, Venice
Watana Charoenrath, AIA, Los Angeles
Annie Chu + Rick Gooding, Los Angeles
Henry N. Cobb, New York
Francesco Dal Co, Venice, Milan
Daly Genik, Los Angeles
Jeff Daniels, AIA, Los Angeles
Francois deMenil, New York
Gary K. Dempster, AIA, Los Angeles
Neil Denari, Los Angeles
Katherine Diamond, FAIA, Los Angeles
Deborah K. Dietsch, Editor-in-Chief, Architecture Magazine, Washington DC
Daniel Mann Johnson & Mendenhall, (DMJM), Los Angeles
Gunther Domenig, Graz
Daniel L. Dworsky, FAIA, Los Angeles
Steven Ehrlich, FAIA, Santa Monica
Peter Eisenman, New York
Julie Eizenberg + Hank Koning, Santa Monica
Merrill Elam, Atlanta
John Enright, Morphosis, Santa Monica
William H. Fain, Jr., FAIA, Los Angeles
Thomas M. Farrage, Culver City
Kristin Feireiss, Berlin
Frederick Fisher, Los Angeles

Allen Don Fong, Fong & Associates, Inc., Costa Mesa
James Ingo Freed, New York
Mickey & Martin Friedman, New York
Craig Hodgetts + Hsin-Ming Fung, Santa Monica
Yokio Futagawa, Tokyo
Yoshio Futagawa, Tokyo
Francesca Garcia-Marques, Associate AIA, Marina del Rey
Sherri Geldin, Columbus
Gensler Architecture, Planning, Design Worldwide, Los Angeles
Joseph Giovannini, New York
Jonathan Glancey, Architecture & Design Editor, The Independent, London
Jorge Glusberg, Buenos Aires
Ron Goldman, FAIA, Los Angeles
Vera Graaf, Architektur & Wohnen, New York
Angéli/Graham Architecture, Los Angeles, Zurich
David Lawrence Gray, FAIA, Santa Monica
Elyse Grinstein, Los Angeles
Kim Groves, Morphosis, Santa Monica
Zaha Hadid, London
Bob Hale, Los Angeles
Hugh Hardy, HHP, New York, Los Angeles
Gisue Hariri & Mojgan Hariri, New York
Robert S. Harris, FAIA, Los Angeles
Laurie Hawkinson/Henry Smith-Miller, New York
David Hertz, AIA, Santa Monica
Thomas Hines, Los Angeles
Marc Hinshaw, San Francisco
Neil Hoffman, Los Angeles
Steven Holl, New York
Hans Hollein, Vienna
Wilhelm Holzbauer, Vienna
Malcolm Holzman, HHP, New York, Los Angeles
Frank E. Hotchkiss, AIA, Laguna Niguel
Michael Hricak, FAIA, Los Angeles
Ishler Design + Engineering Associates, Santa Monica
Arata Isozaki, Tokyo
Helmut Jahn, Chicago
Dominique Jakob, Paris
Charles Jencks, London
David Jenkins, Editorial Director, Phaidon Press, London
The Jerde Partnership International, Inc., Los Angeles
Carlos Jimenez, Houston
Philip Johnson, New York
Steve Johnson/James Favaro, Los Angeles
Scott Johnson, FAIA, Los Angeles

Aleks Istanbullu John Kaliski, Architecture and City Design, Santa Monica
Ray Kappe, Pacific Palisades
Richard Keating, FAIA, Los Angeles
Carol Soucek King, Los Angeles
Jeffrey Kipnis, Columbus
Pierre Koenig, FAIA, Los Angeles
Fred Koetter, New Haven
Rem Koolhaas, Rotterdam
Richard Koshalek, Los Angeles
Phyllis Lambert, Montreal
Lubowicki/Lanier Architects, El Segundo
Sylvia Lavin, Los Angeles
Steven D. Lavine, Los Angeles
Ricardo Legoretta, Mexico City
Michael B. Lehrer, AIA, Los Angeles
Lars Lerup, Houston
Andrew Liang, Form Zero Architectural Books + Gallery, Santa Monica
Prof. Daniel Libeskind, BDA, Berlin
Los Angeles Forum for Architecture and Urban Design, Los Angeles
Richard Cutts Lundquist, Los Angeles
Frank Lupo, New York
Greg Lynn, New York
Susan Kolatan/William J. MacDonald, New York
Brendan MacFarlane, Paris
Rudolpho Machado, Boston
Mark Mack, Venice
Fumihiko Maki, Tokyo
Robert Mangurian + Mary Ann Ray, Culver City
Ira Mann, Los Angeles
Antonina Markoff, Los Angeles
David Martin, FAIA, Los Angeles
Christopher C. Martin, AIA, Los Angeles
Thom & Blythe Mayne, Santa Monica
Mark McVay, Los Angeles
Richard Meier, NYC/Los Angeles
Carl F. Meyer, AIA, Los Angeles
David Michaels, AIA, Los Angeles
Sigrid Miller Pollin, Pomona
Enric Miralles & Benedetta Tagliabue, Barcelona
Rafael Moneo, Madrid
Alan Morishige, AIA, Los Angeles
Morphosis, Santa Monica
David Morton, New York
Eric Owen Moss, Culver City
Professor John V. Mutlow, FAIA, Los Angeles
Herbert Nadel, Los Angeles
Louis Naidorf, FAIA, Los Angeles
Susan Narduli, Venice
Robert Nasraway, AIA, Los Angeles

Doreen Nelson, Los Angeles
David J. Neuman, FAIA, Palo Alto
Robert L Newsom, AIA, Los Angeles
Ben Nicholson, Chicago
Peter Noever, Director MAK - Austrian Museum of Applied Arts, Vienna
Craig S. Norman, AIA, Los Angeles
Merry Norris, Los Angeles
Enrique Norten, Mexico City
Lorcan P. O'Herlihy, Santa Monica
Ove Arup & Partners, Los Angeles
Prof. A. Papadakis, London
Ki Suh Park, FAIA Managing Partner, Gruen Associates, Los Angeles
William Pederson, New York
Norman Pfeiffer, H.H.P.,New York, Los Angeles
Barton Phelps, FAIA, Los Angeles
Renzo Piano, Genoa
Pollari x Somol, Los Angeles
James S. Polshek, FAIA, New York
Elizabeth Moule & Stefanos Polyzoides, Architects and Urbanists, Los Angeles
James F. Porter, AIA, Los Angeles
Peter Pran, Seattle
Antoine Predock, Albuquerque
Michaele Pride-Wells, Lexington
Wolf D. Prix, Coop Himmelb(l)au, Vienna
Rob Quigley, San Diego
George Ranalli, New York
George Rand, Los Angeles
Hani Rashid/Lise Anne Couture, New York
Clifford L. Ratkovich, Los Angeles
Thomas and Carol McMichael Reese, Los Angeles
Mark Rios, Los Angeles
Tony Robbins, Vancouver
Ian F. Robertson, Santa Monica
Darrell S. Rockefeller, AIA, Los Angeles
Richard Rogers, London
Robert Rosenberg, AIA, Los Angeles
Michael Franklin Ross, AIA, Santa Monica
Michael Rotondi, ROTO Architects Inc., Los Angeles
Stephen D. Rountree, Los Angeles
Paul Rudolph, New York
Ceilo + Rey Sacilioc and Robert Naraway, AIA, Los Angeles
Michele Saee, Los Angeles
Stanley Saitowitz, San Francisco
Linda Sanders, Cal Poly Pomona, Pomona
Adèle Naudé Santos, Berkeley
Richard Schlagman, Chairman, Phaidon Press, London
Frederic Schwartz, New York
Josh Schweitzer, Los Angeles

Mack Scogin, Atlanta
Denise Scott Brown, Philadelphia
Erik Sharp, AIA, Los Angeles
Michael Shea, AIA, Los Angeles
Abby Sher, Los Angeles
Jorge Silvetti, Boston
The Partners of Skidmore, Owings, & Merrill, Chicago, New York, San Francisco, London, Washington DC, Los Angeles
Elizabeth A.T. Smith, Los Angeles
Hak Sik Son, Seoul, Santa Monica
Michael Sorkin, New York
SCI-Arc, Piaya del Rey
Laurinda Spear, FAIA, Coral Gables
John Spohrer, Los Angeles
Donald J. Stastny, Portland
Karen D. Stein, New York
Robert A.M. Stern, New York
Clark Stevens, ROTO Architects Inc., Los Angeles
William Stout, San Francisco
Eul-Ho Suh, Seoul
Elizabeth Sverbeyeff Byron, Art & Architecture Editor, Elle Decor Magazine, New York
Helmut Swkzinsky, Coop Himmelb(l)au, Vienna
Shin Takamatsu, Kyoto
Ted T. Tanaka, FAIA, Marina del Rey
Stanley Tigerman, Chicago
UCLA Departement of Architecture + Urban Design, Los Angeles
U.S.C. School of Architecture Faculty, Los Angeles
Susana Torre, New York
Elias Torres, TUR, Barcelona
Bernard Tschumi, New York
Max Underwood, Tempe
Philippe Uzzan, Paris
Karen Van Lengen, New York
Johannes Van Tilburg, FAIA, Santa Monica
Robert Venturi, Philadelphia
Anthony Vidler, Ithaca, NYC
John Walsh, Los Angeles
Edina Weinstein, Santa Monica
Richard Weinstein, Santa Monica
Lorraine Wild, Los Angeles
Tod Williams/Billie Tsien, New York
Tomko Woll Group, Los Angeles
Lebbeus Woods, New York
Eui-Sung Yi, Seoul
Brian S. Yoo, Los Angeles
George C.C. Yu, Vancouver
Buzz Yudell, FAIA, Los Angeles
Paul Zajfen, Los Angeles

THOM MAYNE:

I think my instinct in supporting the design wasn't literally based on the specifics of the building itself... it's really about representing the artistic freedom and expression of an architect... acting on dreams and aspirations and potentialities...that seemed from the onset somewhat unrealizable.

The piece of work realized is something that is benefitting the whole architectural community...it lifts the bar. And I think that most architects realize this.... Finally the city's well-known architects—all very different—are all now reaching the public work—it's huge."

ADVERTISEMENT IN THE
LOS ANGELES TIMES
MARCH 4, 1997

endorsed Gehry and the Concert Hall project. The ad's organizer, Thom Mayne, principal of the Santa Monica-based architecture firm Morphosis, recognized the building's importance for architecture and culture, and for the city of Los Angeles, and encouraged architects to speak out in support of the project.[93] To raise funds for the advertisement, he first contacted the local architectural community and then reached out to the East Coast. The response was immediate. Even major architects who did not like Gehry's building contributed.[94] Mayne also enlisted the support of architects around the world, as he felt it was extremely important to acknowledge the city's global culture and its position as a "mecca for architecture."[95] Coming at a low point for the project, the advertisement also raised the spirits of supporters, especially Lillian Disney.[96]

The strongest backing for the building came in the form of Gehry's own work. In 1996, reports began circulating about an architectural marvel taking place in Bilbao, Spain. When the Guggenheim Museum Bilbao opened in October 1997, it was declared a masterpiece and an instant landmark; Gehry and the industrial port city in northern Spain soon became household names. As Muschamp observed, people now recognized Gehry as an architect who could bring a major project like the Guggenheim in on time and on budget, regardless of his work's ability to arouse a range of associations and projections.[97] And the best news was that the one-hundred-million-dollar Guggenheim Museum was entirely the product of the Gehry office, which designed and completed all of its own construction drawings. Bilbao, finally, was the proof that Los Angeles's civic leaders needed that Walt Disney Concert Hall could be built.

NEW CIVIC LEADERSHIP

As much as any single factor, a leadership vacuum in Los Angeles caused the delay in building Walt Disney Concert Hall. By the mid-1990s the great philanthropic business leaders active in the 1970s and 1980s—the Franklin Murphys, the Robert Andersons, the Edward Carters, the Thorton Bradshaws, the Carl Hartnacks—were gone and no one had truly replaced them yet. The delay in the project allowed time for new leadership in Los Angeles to emerge.

Then-mayor Richard Riordan and his friend Eli Broad, then-chief executive of SunAmerica and a major art collector, joined forces in 1996 to save the project, which one potential donor labeled a "black hole."[98] The mayor and Broad arranged fund-raising meetings with prospective contributors over "many breakfasts, lunches, and dinners," and were able to initiate corporate and business interest in the project. In March 1997, they launched a fund-raising campaign called "The Heart of the City."[99] The Concert Hall supporters now looked to its importance as an agent and beacon of urban revitalization in the Downtown core. "I see Disney Hall as one of seven pearls in a new Downtown necklace," Riordan said in a statement. "Disney Hall will be a major part of the renaissance of the heart of the city."[100] Broad, who was later appointed chairman of the project's oversight committee, saw the Concert Hall within a larger urban context and part

93 Thom Mayne, interview by authors, Santa Monica,
CA, 6 November 2002.
94 Ibid.
95 Ibid.
96 Miller, interview.

97 Herbert Muschamp, "The Miracle in Bilbao,"
New York Times Magazine (7 September 1997): 57.
98 Eli Broad, interview by authors, Westwood, CA, 14 October 2002.
99 Broad, interview; Diane Haithman, "Disney Hall Hangs Its
Pitch on the Future of Downtown," Los Angeles Times, 11 March 1997.
100 Haithman, "Disney Hall Hangs Its Pitch."

JAMES GLYMPH:

The story of Disney Hall is complicated because Disney Hall is old and new. And basically a lot of it is old technology. What we've been able to do with the computer—what we could do at the beginning of Disney and what we do today, the way we did the documents and the computer models for even the current iteration of Disney—are different things because the technology has been evolving during the entire fifteen-year life of the Concert Hall.

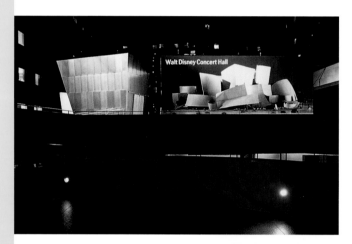

EXTERIOR AND INTERIOR VIEWS
OF THE EXHIBITION
"WALT DISNEY CONCERT HALL:
A CELEBRATION OF MUSIC
AND ARCHITECTURE"
(SHOWN AT THE MUSEUM
OF CONTEMPORARY ART,
LOS ANGELES, FROM OCTOBER 27
TO APRIL 27, 1997)

CRAIG WEBB:

Nobody at that point had ever built a building like this at this scale; it's a very big building. There's a lot of complexity to it…. We were also introducing the use of CATIA, which is the surface modeling program that we use to make shapes.

of a future cultural corridor. He stated: "It wasn't about Disney Hall. It was really about the city.... No one seems to care about the center, the hub of the city, the Downtown. And we said no city can be great today or in world history without a vibrant hub or center."[101] The County had requested a fund-raising plan for the estimated $264.9 million needed for the hall, and the goals were to raise $52 million by July 1997, $89 million by December 1997, and $142 million the next year.[102] By the end of 1997, they had brought the fund-raising total to $168 million—almost double the stated goal—with the help of many new contributors, among them, Mark Willes of the Times Mirror Company, Mike Bowlin of Atlantic Richfield Company, Ron Burkle of Ralphs/Food 4 Less, David Coulter of Bank of America, and Paul Hazen of Wells Fargo. To the credit of Music Center chairman Andrea van de Kamp and community leader Stanley Gold, the year concluded with stunning news: The Walt Disney Company, which up to this time had not pledged any funds to the project, planned to make a challenge gift of $25 million, with a first matching gift from Roy E. and Patti Disney—another major step toward the full financing of the project.[103]

Just as its financial prospects were dramatically revived, Walt Disney Concert Hall headed toward another crisis. In response to constant pressure to lower costs, the Concert Hall's fund-raising leaders contemplated a "design/build" process in which other firms would complete the design and working drawings, with the building's design architect relegated to a consulting role. In June 1997, Gehry balked and announced that he was willing to leave the project. Then an important early supporter stepped in. Diane Disney Miller had played a prominent role in the early planning and served as the family's spokesperson throughout the project. She and her sister Sharon Lund acted resolutely in late 1992 as the Walt Disney Concert Hall Committee debated the question of fast-tracking. Miller stated: "It was our job to support this project."[104] Learning five years later that Gehry's design could be compromised, Miller was furious. She intervened at once to ensure the architect's continued participation. She arranged for dedicated funds from the Disney family to pay Gehry's office to complete the working drawings (Gehry donated his time through the end of construction).[105] From that point on, it was agreed that she would co-chair a new oversight committee. "We promised Los Angeles a Frank Gehry building, and that's what we intend to deliver," she said.[106] Her stalwartness, tenacity, and imagination—characteristics she shared with her father—guaranteed that Walt Disney Concert Hall would remain true to the vision of the architect.

101 Nicolai Ouroussoff, "Bringing Business and Art Together for Disney Hall," *Los Angeles Times*, 18 May 1997.
102 Haithman, "Disney Hall Seeks Funds."
103 Broad, interview; Diane Haithman, "Disney Gives $25 Million to Downtown Concert Hall," Los Angeles Times, 2 December 1997; Bernard Weintraub, "Disney Concert Hall Gets a Pledge," *New York Times*, 2 December 1997.

104 Miller, interview.
105 Giovannini, "Disney Hall and Gehry in Deal."
106 Ibid.

CONCLUSION

In the end, what matters most, of course, extends beyond the people and details of its making to the future life of the building itself. Walt Disney Concert Hall will engage audiences with the greatest ideas in music and architecture. The space of the Concert Hall—where, as Weinstein notes, "you feel the joy of creation in the work itself"[107]—will challenge conductors and musicians to rise to another level of performance, as Pierre Boulez, Zubin Mehta, Isaac Stern, and others have said of the world's great concert halls. Walt Disney Concert Hall will be transformational both for the Los Angeles Philharmonic, inspiring them to be daring, and for the city, becoming what Deborah Borda terms a "convener" of intellectual thought and discussion.[108]

It is a building, therefore, that links abstractly, yet potently to the vision of its namesake. As was noted years ago during the architecture competition, Gehry is perhaps the one architect alive whose imagination has so much in common with Walt Disney's. His work gives a sense of wonder and delight with serious undertones, "just what we got as kids from Disney movies."[109] Like Disney, Gehry has an intuitive ability to understand what people want, with an immediacy that connects to all types of people.[110] Finally, Walt Disney Concert Hall is what Lillian Disney envisioned and more: a concert hall with outstanding acoustics and a garden in the heart of the Los Angeles—symbolic of the city's hard-earned achievement and the worthy struggle to realize works of creativity that can communicate intuitively for all time. We feel that, without any doubt, Walt Disney Concert Hall is the most astonishing masterpiece of public architecture ever built in Los Angeles.

107 Weinstein, interview.
108 Deborah Borda, interview by authors, Los Angeles, 18 December 2002.
109 Walsh, "Walt Disney Concert Hall Committee Report," 5 December 1988. Frank Gehry met Walt Disney around 1962 when Pereira, Luckman, Williams had a joint venture to design the Los Angeles International Airport. The group had brought in Walt Disney to discuss the idea of building a small version of Disneyland near LAX's theme building. Disney said it was a bad idea—if the venture succeeded, there would be terrible traffic problems. Gehry recalls, "I remember I liked him and I didn't expect to." (Frank Gehry, interview by authors, Santa Monica, 26 November 2002).
110 Weinstein, interview.

ERNEST FLEISCHMANN:

A hall gives an orchestra its soul, its character....
This is the first time the musicians will be playing in the same
room as the audience. With a proscenium stage there
is a kind of psychological curtain between the performers
and the audience, and that's going to be removed.

from left: ESA-PEKKA SALONEN,
FRANK GEHRY, FRED STEGEMAN,
YASUHISA TOYOTA, ERNEST
FLEISCHMANN, FRED NICHOLAS,
AND CRAIG WEBB, AT THE
GEHRY STUDIO, 1993

ELI BROAD:

We have demonstrated to the people of Los Angeles—
who do not always believe that they've got a great city
or believe they can accomplish great things—that great
things can be done, that there is some civic leadership
out there. We don't have a tradition of philanthropy,
but perhaps this is the beginning.

from left: ESA-PEKKA SALONEN,
FRANK GEHRY AND
ERNEST FLEISCHMANN
AT THE GEHRY STUDIO,
1993

2.2.00

9.8.00

3.20.01

8.30.01

10.5.00

12.27.00

7.23.02

3.22.03

ELI BROAD:

*Cities are remembered by their art and culture, but cities can
support only one great symphony, one great opera; in Los Angeles they
all come together Downtown. This is why Disney Hall is so important.
Architecture is the mother of the arts, and quality architecture
raises our level of self-respect and demand for quality in other things.*

Carol McMichael Reese

All Shiny and New:
WALT DISNEY CONCERT HALL
and the
REHABILITATION *of*
DOWNTOWN LOS ANGELES

Walt Disney Concert Hall occupies the corner of Grand Avenue and First Street in the section of Los Angeles most familiarly known as "Downtown." It is a daring building and a dazzling object that the rational mind understands as inert—of stone, steel, and glass. But instinctively we react to the Concert Hall as if it were energized with something akin to a life force. It bursts onto the scene with such vivacity that it creates a continual urban celebration, like a Fourth of July fireworks display with a limitless supply of incendiary devices. Reflected light radiates in all directions from its stainless steel cladding, with walls that cant up and out, moving away from plumb in multiple directions and at different angles. The building pushes against the confines of its corner lot, seeming to elbow its way onto the sidewalk and out into the intersection. Walt Disney Concert Hall brings life to the streets from which it rises with a shining burst of optimism in the future of Los Angeles as a city. It causes us to think, as we perhaps have not thought collectively in a long time, about Downtown Los Angeles and the ways in which it represents not only the communal joys and advantages but also the frustrations and challenges of living in a metropolis that is one of the fastest growing and most environmentally precarious in the world.

When Walt Disney Concert Hall opens in late 2003, the project to build it will have lasted sixteen years, but the forces behind it—forces that produced a building dedicated to the performance of symphonic music in a highly visible downtown district devoted to the arts—have gathered momentum for a century.[1] The Concert Hall is the result of longstanding dreams to make

1 This essay is dedicated to Ernest Fleischmann, managing director of the Los Angeles Philharmonic, 1969-98, and lifetime member of the Board of Directors, and Frederick M. Nicholas, chair of the Walt Disney Concert Hall Committee, 1987-94.

Downtown the symbol of the city's collective enterprise by locating flagship buildings for government, commerce, and culture there. And, in the face of equally longstanding processes of metropolitan decentralization and disintegration, these dreams continue to drive hopes that the Concert Hall will have a regenerative effect on Downtown. To understand what the Concert Hall might mean for the renewal of Downtown, we must revisit past proposals for revitalizing Los Angeles's urban core. This essay looks at some of the most historically important plans for Downtown's public center that were authored in the last century by architects, urban planners, and citizen commissions, and it relates them to ideas about the city that the Concert Hall's design proposes. Of particular interest are those schemes that have failed, been controversial, or only partially succeeded. Herbert Muschamp, architecture critic for the *New York Times*, recently urged readers to take unbuilt designs for the urban sphere seriously, as "special causes,…links in the chain of causality that produces, sustains, and transforms major cities over time."[2] In the belief that familiarity with the history of the various visions for remaking Downtown Los Angeles might strengthen the groundswell that the opening of the Concert Hall has occasioned, it seems an opportune moment to review the special causes relative to improving Downtown Los Angeles that have been put forward during the twentieth century and that proponents of a revitalized Downtown passionately support today.

A description of Downtown as encompassed by a ring of freeways (the 110 Harbor/Pasadena to the west, the 101 Hollywood/Santa Ana to the north and east, and the 10 Santa Monica to the south) provides a shorthand explanation of its mapped framework, but with an important proviso. Just beyond the northeastern edge of the distinctive freeway ring lies the site of the city's eighteenth-century birthplace. Its amputation from the newer districts of Downtown by highway construction fiat and the building of the 101 freeway in the 1940s and 1950s is one of the great shames of California transportation planning. This historic sector, which now includes El Pueblo de Los Angeles, Chinatown, and the transportation hub around Union Station, is integral to understanding Los Angeles's conception of itself and must be considered the "Downtown" as well. Although the freeways severed the older center of the city from its newer counterpart, Downtown's center of gravity comprises both. Many continually struggle to suture the rend in the tissue of the city's heart because Los Angeles's urban memories, government buildings, and cultural institutions are gathered here to sustain some form of urban identity, however fragile or ephemeral.

In the early twenty-first century, Downtown is a microcosm of the "prismatic metropolis" that Los Angeles has become.[3] In the city of Los Angeles, the *US Census 2000* reported a population of approximately 3.5 million, of which 40.9 percent are foreign-born and 57.8 percent speak a language other than English at home. Developing a unitary "civic center" with buildings assumed to be symbolic of shared civic values is more challenging today in increasingly heterogeneous Los Angeles, or, for that matter, in any other globalizing city. Competing, or at least multi-present centers represent a number of ethnicities Downtown. Chinatown, Little Tokyo, and Koreatown have all achieved the physical status of Downtown enclaves. The Latino population of Los Angeles, although strongly represented Downtown in an entrenched retail district along

2 Herbert Muschamp, "A See-Through Library of Shifting Shapes and Colors," *New York Times*, 19 January 2003.

3 Lawrence D. Bobo et al., eds., *Prismatic Metropolis, Inequality in Los Angeles* (New York: Russell Sage Foundation, 2000).

Broadway, still has not established an honorific core there—unless one counts El Pueblo de Los Angeles State Historic Park (where the Latino Museum of History, Art, and Culture has considered relocating), which is organized around the early nineteenth-century Spanish colonial Los Angeles Plaza and includes the commercialized and touristic Olvera Street district. Downtown also boasts a financial core of skyscrapers; a convention center with a relatively new sports arena; a market district specializing in flowers, produce, groceries, toys, small electronics, clothing, and other wholesale goods; a district of historic theaters and commercial structures; and several districts of new housing added over the last forty years. Walt Disney Concert Hall takes its place in the Los Angeles Civic Center, the group of monumental government and cultural buildings that were erected after decades of struggle and controversy on Bunker Hill, Downtown's most conspicuous land mass. Here, the Concert Hall stands both as the result of a persistent consensus that Downtown should boast a concentrated, contiguous cultural district and as a new rallying point for the achievement of that urban goal.

This essay focuses on the past century's dreams of building out Bunker Hill as an acropolis for Los Angeles. In many ways, Bunker Hill is the heart of the heart of the city.[4] Walt Disney Concert Hall was sited very consciously on Bunker Hill in relation to a number of arts venues: the Central Library (Bertram Goodhue, 1926), the three theaters of the Music Center (Welton Beckett and Associates, 1964), the Museum of Contemporary Art, Los Angeles (MOCA) (Arata Isosaki, 1987), and the Richard D. Colburn School of the Performing Arts (Hardy, Holzman, Pfeiffer, 1998). The Concert Hall's urban influence, which most believe will be significant, will be most strongly felt in the Bunker Hill district of Downtown. However, since the Concert Hall is prominently associated with what many see as the current resurgence of larger Downtown, it is worth surveying the urban context beyond the hall's immediate neighborhood to learn what is at issue for the city's core. Although the Concert Hall was conceived in an era when monumentality was considered the key design feature for achieving civic identity, in today's Los Angeles—bursting with diversity—an imagery of connectivity is also necessary for representing the civic realm. Walt Disney Concert Hall achieves both. It is simultaneously a solitary, outstanding "figure," and a convivial, contributing presence inscribed in the "ground" of the city's fabric.

WALT DISNEY CONCERT HALL'S GENETIC CODE FOR URBAN REVITALIZATION

The Walt Disney Concert Hall Committee, which oversaw the design development of the building until the mid-1990s, insisted in the 1988 competition brief that architects competing for the commission demonstrate an "understanding of the Walt Disney Concert Hall as a 'building block' of the city."[5] Thus a genetic code for stimulating urban renaissance was written into the conception of the Concert Hall from the outset. Frank Gehry won the commission, in part, because he understood better than his competitors the life-enhancing effect on Downtown that such genetic material could have. Over the decade-long

4 William H. Gass, *In the Heart of the Heart of the Country and Other Stories* (Boston: David R. Godine, 1981, rev. ed.).

5 Carol McMichael Reese and Thomas Ford Reese, "Böhm, Gehry, Hollein, and Stirling in Los Angeles," *Zodiac 2* (1989): 157.

design process, he never failed to take into account the Concert Hall Committee's insistence that his building fulfill a civic responsibility to enhance the public realm of its Downtown site.

One telling Gehry drawing in the archive of documents related to the design for Walt Disney Concert Hall vividly communicates the architect's grasp of the urban possibilities. It is a plan drawing in black pen on white paper, worked in Gehry's full, swift line, that was produced as a study during the competition stage of the project (figure 1). At this early stage, Gehry drew not only the Concert Hall's site—the Bunker Hill block bounded by Grand Avenue on the east, Hope Street on the west, First Street on the north, and Second Street on the south (bottom block on the drawing)—but also the vacant County-owned lots to the east (middle and top blocks). Significantly, he drew concentric wave patterns around the hall that radiated from its welcoming lobby, which he insightfully described on another drawing as a "living room for the city." The waves are perhaps transcriptions of sound flowing over the street, and they break across the terrace and sidewalk, billowing out across Grand Avenue from the Concert Hall site toward the empty blocks, which the competing architects were asked to address in their proposals. Importantly, this key process drawing signifies Gehry's conception of the Concert Hall's role as a primary instigator in the urban renewal process.

However compelling Gehry's response, the mandate for the Concert Hall's urban challenge lay with the building's clients. Walt Disney Concert Hall was intended to enlarge the Music Center—officially, the Performing Arts Center of Los Angeles County. The construction of the Music Center atop Bunker Hill in 1964 had developed formerly "empty" land that had been razed at the end of the 1950s to address Downtown "blight." Sited on a parcel that had been cleared almost thirty years earlier but was still not redeveloped, the Concert Hall project continued that urban renewal trajectory. Thus, it is not surprising that the Concert Hall Committee's competition brief expressed impressive, far-reaching urban goals. Their instructions urged not only that the Concert Hall "convey a unifying theme...[and] compliment the Music Center," but that it also "strongly influence the quality of design and construction of adjacent projects...[and] create a major cultural corridor on Grand Avenue." In their charge to competitors, then, the Concert Hall Committee boldly fostered dialogue about the improvement of Downtown. The public rhetoric of Downtown revitalization has crystallized around the Concert Hall since at least late 1995, when efforts to fund the building's escalating costs and to restart its stalled construction began. The information packet assembled for the purpose of raising additional donations to its coffers was titled "The Heart of the City," and its most prominent champions integrated that clarion call in their appeals. They also joined a century-old civic discussion about the ways in which the physical environment of Downtown—its streets, buildings, parks, and landscaping—could serve as prominent symbols of aspirations to promote the common good.

BACK TO THE FUTURE
OF DOWNTOWN LOS ANGELES

The earliest concerted effort to rebuild Downtown Los Angeles took place in the first decade of the twentieth century, when Angelenos commissioned nationally recognized urban improvement consultant Charles Mulford Robinson to prepare a plan for the recuperation of the city's center (figure 2). One hundred years ago, the stimulus for urban renewal in Los Angeles and other cities in the United States was the

1. FRANK GEHRY,
PLAN SKETCH FOR LOTS K
(CONCERT HALL SITE),
Q, AND W-2 ON
BUNKER HILL, 1989

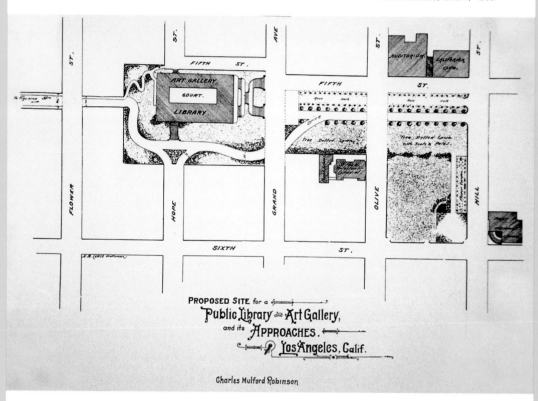

2. CHARLES MULFORD ROBINSON,
"PROPOSED SITE FOR
A PUBLIC LIBRARY AND ART GALLERY
AND ITS APPROACHES,
LOS ANGELES, CALIF.," 1909

ROBERT S. HARRIS:
Disney Hall is like a catcher's mitt.
It has the potential to make a genuine cultural
impact. Gehry had important ideas about
how to make a cultural institution accessible
to the public at large. He opened up the
whole site so that people can move around it,
through the gardens, up to the top
of the building, and attend free events in
the amphitheater.

enhancement of Washington, DC, an effort that was publicized and discussed nationwide. The 1902 scheme, known as the Senate Park Commission Plan, reorganized the National Mall as a luxuriantly planted field that would provide a suitable ground for the classically-inspired temples of science, history, art, and democratic governance that were expected to line its edges. The publication of the Senate Park Commission Plan stimulated the nascent City Beautiful movement, a national drive for urban improvement in the face of increased industrialization and immigration, and "civic improvement expert" Charles Mulford Robinson was its foremost proponent.

The progressive political and social tenor of the era is well captured in the book published by Los Angeles preacher and settlement-house worker Dana Bartlett, *The Better City: A Sociological Study of a Modern City* (1907), which promoted addressing the needs of the city's immigrants, orphans, elderly, and working poor through organized societies and other community efforts. Bartlett's "better" or "greater" Los Angeles was to be a city that would "concentrate thought upon the ethical ideal—believing that a city may become noted for its righteousness, its morality, its social virtues, its artistic life as for its material resources."[6] In the same year that Bartlett's book was published, the Los Angeles Municipal Art Commission invited Robinson to give advice about a "better Los Angeles." Robinson's published report, *Los Angeles, California: The City Beautiful* (1909), called for the "redemption of Los Angeles, its rebuilding along splendid lines...to pull together for the city's good."[7] The framework of Robinson's improvement plan for Los Angeles was the design of three urban districts that were to crystallize its image as a "great city." First, he recommended a transportation nexus around a new union railroad station to enhance the experience of entering and leaving the urban core. Second, he planned an administrative or civic center, to centralize the buildings that housed the civic government, and thus to give prominent visibility to the city as the locus of democracy. Third, he envisioned a cultural center to magnify the effect of what was then known as Central Park—today, Pershing Square—by locating a new library and art gallery nearby. Each of these districts was to make apparent to all who worked and lived in Los Angeles, as well as to those who visited there, that the urban environment offered the best of modern amenities. Even more important, the symbolic value of the whole was more than the sum of these separate districts, because their aggregate effect was to persuade citizens that building the city anew was a necessary and noble undertaking.

Just as the 1902 Senate Park Commission Plan was adopted as a guide for the building of the core of Washington, DC, so a consensus formed around Robinson's 1909 plan for Los Angeles, which resulted in the eventual development of a cultural center, a public transportation hub, and a civic center. Only the cultural center arose in the exact location that Robinson had recommended. It began to take shape when Bertram Goodhue's boldly geometric Central Library (1926) was sited, as Robinson had suggested, at the southern foot of Bunker Hill. The library, which is one of Los Angeles's most important early twentieth-century buildings, sowed the seeds of the blossoming Grand Avenue cultural corridor that the Concert Hall now crowns. The library's impressive tower looked expectantly across Fifth Street toward Bunker Hill, and its eastern wing containing the children's reading room and courtyard garden stretched toward Grand Avenue. Walt Disney Concert Hall renews the currency of Robinson's plan for Los Angeles—not in the latter's

6 Dana W. Bartlett, preface to *The Better City: A Sociological Study of a Modern City* (Los Angeles: Neuner Company, 1907).

7 Charles Mulford Robinson, "Report of the Municipal Art Commission," in *Los Angeles, California: The City Beautiful* (Los Angeles: William J. Porter, 1909), n. p.

details, but rather in its special cause, which called for prominent focal points within the core that would be linked by landscaped boulevards. Today, the Concert Hall's generous, exuberant Grand Avenue staircase reaches out to the southeast and its nearer neighbors, MOCA and the Colburn School. The Concert Hall also makes a sweeping urban gesture to the northeast with its entrance plaza that opens diagonally to the corner of Grand Avenue and First Street, where the Music Center meets the Civic Center.

GREENING THE CITY'S CORE ON BUNKER HILL

Decisions about the location of the Civic Center and the Music Center in relation to Bunker Hill mark the second historical phase of Los Angeles's Downtown renewal process and opened the site that Walt Disney Concert Hall now so compellingly occupies. Although citizens who worked to improve the city—including the mayor-appointed Municipal Art Commission that hired Charles Mulford Robinson as a consultant— were determined to build a civic center, they could not agree on its location. Their disagreements were exacerbated by the fact that the city's commercial center was developing rapidly to the south, away from the historic Plaza. There were numerous opinions, but they can be divided into two camps. One position generally favored Robinson's idea that the Civic Center should be inflected toward the Plaza, along a north-south axis. The opposing position supported the siting of the Civic Center along an east-west axis in relationship to Bunker Hill and with connections to the "new" Downtown. The latter camp included visionaries who saw Bunker Hill's crown as a potential terrace on which could be built a "shining city on the hill." In 1924, the Allied Architects Association, a group of Los Angeles professionals who joined forces for the purpose of securing civic commissions, gave form to that vision, submitting a plan for an "Administration Center for the City and the County of Los Angeles" which proposed building a civic acropolis atop Bunker Hill (figure 3).

In the minds of many early twentieth-century urban improvers, Bunker Hill, a once leafy, prosperous Victorian neighborhood, was ripe for redevelopment, since it had been effectively strangled when prestigious downtown commercial development moved around its perimeter to the south and west, and tunnels were cut beneath it—the Third Street Tunnel, for example, as early as 1900—to carry traffic to burgeoning West Los Angeles (see LA A-2). By the mid-1920s, the predominant urban image of Bunker Hill was that of an increasingly derelict, predominantly residential zone of degraded buildings and entrenched poverty. The basic concept of the Allied Architects' plan was the greening of Bunker Hill. It envisioned wide swaths of multi-block parks stretching west from the Plaza up the slope of Bunker Hill and covering its crown—from the Central Library on the south to historic Fort Moore (dedicated July 4, 1847) on the north. The perimeters of these parks were then designated as sites for buildings in which public business was to be conducted. The plan thus predicted the razing of Bunker Hill as the potential site for buildings that would embody the city's metropolitan image, and it envisioned that the Los Angeles City Hall would be built at the crest of Bunker Hill. Although City Hall (John C. Austin, John and Donald Parkinson, and Albert C. Martin, 1928) was built instead at the bottom of the hill on Main Street, the Allied Architects' plan had an important urban legacy in the development of the Civic Center up the eastern slope of Bunker Hill (named El Paseo on the plan), where today, public buildings line the terraced Civic Center Mall along First and Temple streets between Main Street and Grand Avenue.

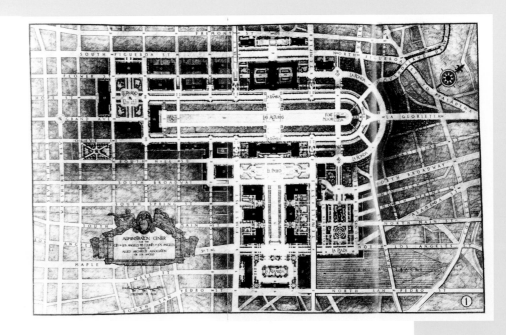

3. ALLIED ARCHITECTS
ASSOCIATION
OF LOS ANGELES,
"ADMINISTRATION
CENTER FOR THE
CITY AND COUNTY
OF LOS ANGELES," 1924

STUART M. KETCHUM:

*Disney Hall will be an unbelievable tourist attraction, and, with the Cathedral
and the Staples Center, will stimulate a major injection into Downtown—
a repeat of the Bilbao phenomenon. Tourists will add Disney Hall to their 'must see'
list of Hollywood, the Pacific Ocean, and Disneyland. But the key to Downtown's
long-term success is more—and denser—housing, with hospitals and schools.*

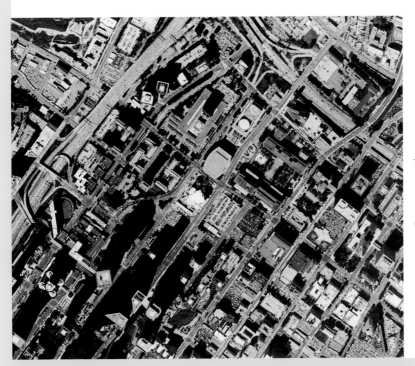

4. AERIAL PHOTOGRAPH
TAKEN FROM THE SOUTH,
SHOWING WALT DISNEY
CONCERT HALL'S SPATIAL
RELATIONSHIP TO THE
CIVIC CENTER MALL, 2003

ZEV YAROSLAVSKY:

*Downtown is a big place, and people don't necessarily want
to be Downtown. There are too many other options here.
People vote and invest with their feet. Downtown, to most voters,
is just another center. But the pieces are starting to come together
in the urban core. It's a time-consuming process to bring people
along. We try to do the right thing after exhausting the alternatives.*

5. GRAND AVENUE
COMMITTEE,
"CIVIC PARK LOOKING
TO CITY HALL,"
2003

JOHN KALISKI:

*Downtown has to make itself more physically appealing—
beyond the first blush of enthusiasm—in order to reach the second
and third levels of residential growth. There is a friction generated
by the needs of the indigent and homeless Downtown and
the emerging residential community there. Catalytic projects like
Disney Hall have to be seen in that context.*

special cause was that of a landscaped "heart of the city," through
...uments, and destinations were to be linked by pedestrian-friendly
...is still promising today, but remains incompletely realized. At either
...l, two stirring works of civic architecture are situated—City Hall
...erraro Building of the Department of Water and Power (DWP) (Albert
...'s apex. Below, City Hall opens broadly toward the Bunker Hill acropolis
...onze doors, its walls emblazoned with the quotation, "The city came
...fe; it exists for the good life." Brought back to prominence through the
...ative Project Restore, which was established in 1986 and headed by
...bert C. Martin, this gleaming, off-white Beaux-Arts civic skyscraper boasts
...e ancient tradition of a lighthouse—the symbolic beacon of a port city.
..., it is a crossroads building, as its portals open to the four streets surround-
...occupies, symbolically gathering to it all comers from the urban territory
...he DWP building is an almost pure exercise in mid-century modernism, with
...d-concrete slabs and vertical steel supports. Its open-bay floors emit light
...h at night, and it shines out above downtown like a gigantic lantern beckoning
...et both the DWP building and City Hall preside over a Mall that is largely
...e to five, Monday through Friday. Understandably, the growing numbers of
...geles have found their way to the public landscape of the Civic Center, and
...and routine purges by law enforcement officers are a deplorable response
...ity.

...y Concert Hall promotes the resuscitation of the Civic Center Mall and
...ening of its green spaces to the city beyond. Brilliantly, Gehry struck the hall's
...ough the block, rather than orienting it exclusively toward the Music Center,
...ornered entrance toward Grand Avenue and the Civic Center Mall. Here,
...olley takes aim at the defensive dike that urban accretions such as entrances
...king garages and various measures against encampments of the homeless
...ound the Mall (figure 4). The Concert Hall alone, however, cannot rehabilitate
...t of the promise of the Concert Hall's urban position, the Music Center spon-
...eld in December of 2000, in which architects Frank Gehry, Arata Isosaki,
...landscape architect Laurie Olin, and real estate developer and Music Center
...art Ketchum participated. This short, intense design charrette studied, among
other issues, the enhancement of connections between the Music Center and the Civic Center
Mall, which the Concert Hall forcefully implies. As a result of the workshop, the Grand Avenue
Committee, a public/private partnership, was formed in 2001. Co-chaired by Downtown developer
James Thomas and self-identified "venture philanthropist" Eli Broad, who has given upwards
of $7 million to the Walt Disney Concert Hall campaign, the committee includes politicians and
public officials as well. They propose to transform the twenty-acre Civic Center Mall into a lively,
twenty-four-hours-a-day, seven-days-a-week public space, which Broad refers to as Los Angeles's
new Central Park (figure 5). Their plans connect the Civic Center Mall at long last with Grand
Avenue, from which it currently is screened off by a drop in elevation and a massive retaining
wall that contains spiral ramps leading to the County's parking garage, which extends under
the Music Center and the Mall itself. In the scheme, a wider sidewalk on the Music Center side
of Grand Avenue, created by shifting the roadbed to the east, offers an improved environment

to pedestrians. A pedestrian bridge over the garage ramps mitigates their obstructive effect until the time when funds may be available to move the ramps to the edges of the park. An outdoor amphitheater sited between the County Hall of Administration (Stanton, Stockwell, Williams, and Wilson; Austin, Field, and Fry, 1956) and the County Courthouse (J. E. Stanton, Paul R. Williams, Adrian Wilson; Austin, Field, and Fry, 1958) accomplishes a visual and physical passage from the Music Center plaza into the park. However, unless Downtown housing provisions are made—whether homeless shelters, or single-room-occupancy and low-income units—and commensurate social services are provided, the promise of City Hall's message is empty, and the Central Park that the Grand Avenue Committee has mobilized to achieve will fail.

ACCOMMODATING RAPID TRANSIT AND MAKING PLACES FOR PEOPLE ON BUNKER HILL

Another scheme for the Los Angeles Civic Center—also produced during the period when its location was under consideration—advanced special causes that are pertinent today as well. This was the 1925 project of Lloyd Wright, Frank Lloyd Wright's oldest son, who lived and practiced in Los Angeles from 1919 until his death in 1978.[8] Like the Allied Architects' plan of the previous year, Wright's plan emphasized the symbolic resonance of public buildings sited atop the Bunker Hill acropolis (figure 6). Wright's plan presciently devoted sites along Grand Avenue to buildings housing the fine arts, from the Central Library grounds to the crown of Bunker Hill. His plan also recommended that City Hall be built in the exact location at the northern apex of Bunker Hill that is now newly occupied by Rafael Moneo's dramatic—and yet serene—Cathedral of Our Lady of the Angels (2002), which presides over the chasm where the Hollywood Freeway (101) cuts through Bunker Hill. However, the contribution of Wright's plan that is especially relevant now lies in the realm of transportation planning and terraced pedestrian street corridors made highly visible with plantings. In suggesting complex, layered, and separated movement systems for vehicles (including airplanes!) and pedestrians throughout the Civic Center site, Wright's plan acknowledged that increasing traffic and congestion were deeply problematic issues for cities. His excavated, rapid-transit throughways predicted the freeway troughs that would be cut around Downtown in the 1940s and 1950s, but Wright discretely buried his vehicular "speedways" under broad terraces where pedestrians had the rights and pleasures of passage.

The lesson to be learned from Wright is particularly relevant to recent proposals for a rehabilitated Grand Avenue, which Walt Disney Concert Hall's opening has stimulated and which the Grand Avenue Committee has pursued. Sweeping north from the Central Library, past MOCA, the Colburn School, the Concert Hall, the Music Center, and the Civic Center, Grand Avenue reaches the Cathedral and the ignominious freeway crossing that separates Downtown from one of Los Angeles's most magnificent urban vantage points—the outcrop on which Fort Moore once perched overlooking the Plaza. Buildings belonging to the Los Angeles Unified School District (formerly housing the Los Angeles Metropolitan High School and, most recently,

8 See "Notable Civic Center Scheme," *Los Angeles Times*, 30 August 1925; see also *Los Angeles Examiner*, 26 November 1926, for Wright's "City of the Future."

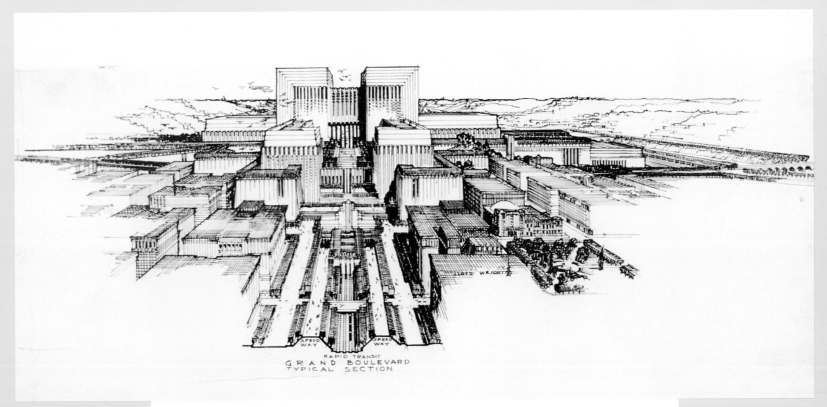

FREDERICK M. NICHOLAS:

*Everyone was at the table, the CRA, the County,
the Music Center, the Philharmonic, the architects;
I met every Monday with the County's lawyer to resolve
issues, and I met every week with the Music Center.
If something is important to a community, it gets done.*

AYAHLUSHIM HAMMOND:

*Disney Hall finally puts Downtown on the map and gives Downtown
something of substance that was missing. Still, we have to ask:
should the focus of Downtown be on creating monuments or connective
tissue? Downtown needs walkable streets, green spaces for loitering
and for children, better transit linkages to Bunker Hill and the historic
core. The lack of resources results in a focus on attracting developers,
rather than on articulating an overall vision.*

Without a vibrant center, the city will be divided. What is needed Downtown is a place
for community celebrations, a Central Park, a commons on the sixteen acres of vacant land
stretching from the Department of Water and Power Building to City Hall.

7. GRAND AVENUE
COMMITTEE,
"GRAND AVENUE
LOOKING SOUTH,"
2003

STEPHEN D. ROUNTREE:

Grand Avenue can be an icon of magnificence, a point of pride.
A recent economic study showed that Los Angeles has 'strong' cultural
resources but a 'weak' brand image as a city. The Grand Avenue
Project can strengthen that image. The Music Center hopes, literally,
to touch the street, to be a part of creating pedestrian street life
that will engage Downtown workers and residents.

the Board of Education) currently occupy the site. Visionary efforts spearheaded by Eli Broad are afoot to create a new magnet high school devoted to the visual and performing arts, on the model of the La Guardia High School of Music & Art and Performing Arts in New York. A limited competition recently named the Viennese firm Coop-Himmelb(l)au the winner of the commission to develop pieces of the project tangential to Grand Avenue. According to plan, the whole site will be returned to a more public use, which will include exhibition and performance spaces. It is expected that tens of thousands will be attracted every year to this spectacular overlook, with its most impressive panoramic view of the Cathedral and the city.

Anticipating this project, the Grand Avenue Committee has explored designs for widening the Grand Avenue bridge over the Hollywood Freeway in order to complete the extension of the arts and culture promenade from one side of the Bunker Hill acropolis to the other. And, in tandem, Julie Silliman, cultural arts planner for the Community Redevelopment Agency (CRA), has commissioned a public arts project for the bridge. Rapid transit, which the freeways were built to provide, need not "shrivel the heart out of Downtown," as Reyner Banham described their overwhelming effect in 1971, if agreement can be reached and investment can be secured to return life-giving flows of pedestrians and local traffic to the center.[9] Wright's concept of three-quarters of a century ago holds out hope today, and the Concert Hall provides the impetus for redesign and remedies for the discontinuities of the Downtown street fabric created by freeways and tunnels. Yet Walt Disney Concert Hall itself requires accommodation along Grand Avenue, which the Grand Avenue Committee's proposals have also addressed. Their plans for curving Grand Avenue away from the Concert Hall and enlarging the sidewalk aprons at the Music Center and the Concert Hall would not only enhance pedestrians' experience of the street but would also give the Concert Hall additional breathing room. The price of realizing these dreams is dear. Nevertheless, there are many dedicated forces at work. The Metropolitan Transportation Authority and Caltrans, for example, have contributed funds for improving Grand Avenue between Second Avenue and Temple Street—from the Concert Hall to the Cathedral—and work is underway, but no one knows at this point where financial support will be found for reworking the street beyond this two-block extent.

The Concert Hall's urban prospects along Grand Avenue are also dependent on the effects of buildings that have not yet been designed for the critical "empty" lots on Bunker Hill that are its immediate neighbors (figure 7). These lots—County-owned Q and W-2, directly east of the Concert Hall, and City-owned L and M-2, on its south—were razed by the CRA in the late 1950s, following its formation under state law in conjunction with the federal Housing Act of 1949. Since Lots Q, L, and M-2 all border Grand Avenue, they are of crucial concern to the Grand Avenue Committee, one of whose goals is to initiate and guide development on them (Lots L and M-2 actually lie below Grand Avenue between Second and Third streets, which tunnel under Bunker Hill; Grand Avenue thus crosses the hill as a bridge structure above them). According to architect Martha Welborne, the committee's managing director, a joint-powers agreement is the best mechanism for insuring that meritorious design guidelines and socially conscious planning are prioritized. A design oversight team is necessary because designating development companies to hire architects and sign tenants could result in an architectural solution of less than excellent quality—millions of square feet will be devoted to multiple uses. Lots L and M-2 are zoned by the

9 Reyner Banham, *Los Angeles, The Architecture of Four Ecologies*
(Harmondsworth, Middlesex, England: Penguin, 1971), 212.

City primarily for housing, with some entertainment and retail functions. While offices are expected to predominate in the 1.5 million square feet of mixed-use space that has been permitted on Lot Q, it will also support residential, commercial, cultural, and entertainment spaces. A novel—at least for Los Angeles—workable team approach is needed, rather than cutthroat real estate practice and fractious City/County politics as usual. The CRA's wholesale destruction of the historic residential district atop Bunker Hill has long been the subject of controversy, and housing activists have demanded an accounting for residential units lost when Bunker Hill was demolished—10,000 people were left without homes—and the addition of new housing in any redevelopment scheme. Indeed, it is possible that civic pride in Walt Disney Concert Hall will help facilitate collaboration and lay this controversy to rest, but only if the issue of providing affordable housing Downtown is finally addressed.

MASTER PLANNING
AND ORGANIC REDEVELOPMENT

If there has been almost a century of consensus regarding the desirability of clustering public institutions around a cultural center and a civic center in Downtown Los Angeles, there has been far more ambivalence about the urban fabric that supports such building groups and endeavors. Public buildings and monuments that are visited by tourists and event-goers and are inhabited by those who work in the city from eight to five do not a vital city center make. The decision to create an acropolis of monuments on Bunker Hill can be traced to master-planning schemes of the City Beautiful era. It was furthered by planners who shared visions of a downtown characterized by a monumental center and notable ensembles of business buildings. This was the prominent position advocated in planning documents such as the Preface to a Master Plan (1941), but also one taken by citizen task forces—such as Greater Los Angeles Plans, Inc. and the Central City Committee—and by Calvin Hamilton, the City's director of planning from 1965 to 1985. However, these initiators and their initiatives recognized the necessity for regional planning on a metropolitan scale, and they also furthered the "centers concept" that supported the development of multiple, high-density centers dispersed from the core, to which lower-density residential neighborhoods would be tethered. The builders of the Music Center, for example, accepted the notion that its theaters would rely on patrons who, for the most part, would commute Downtown to events. While the persistence of this "acropolis complex" may have produced the Concert Hall at its site on Bunker Hill in the late 1980s, it is widely understood almost fifteen years later that the hall's long-term survival as a cultural nexus depends in large measure on the vitality that will swirl around it twenty-four hours a day. Walt Disney Concert Hall is a rallying point rather than a comprehensive solution.

The seeds of revitalized Downtown housing were sown in the master-planning days of the 1970s, when CRA's "Central Business District Redevelopment Project" (1972)—known as the "Silver Book Plan" because of the color of its cover—guided renewal. The plan emphasized the achievement of a "balanced environment" through political and economic provisions for low- and moderate-income housing, which has been the CRA's mandate since its founding. Detractors of the Silver Book Plan have argued, however, that although it guided the clearance of "blight," it saw too little below-market-rate housing replaced, leaving Downtown more housing-poor and income-segregated than ever. Robert S. Harris, a professor of architecture and urban design at the University of Southern California who has lived downtown since 1990, agrees that strong residential neighborhoods will insure Downtown's vitality, particularly by increasing the number of stakeholders who vote on related issues.

If voters are to be engaged in planning and architectural issues, they must be presented with full documentary portfolios that include images as well as words and numbers. Intelligently and persuasively, the two committees that undertook major planning efforts for Downtown in the wake of the Silver Book Plan published comprehensive sets of images of their proposals. The special cause of the packaging of both these plans was the dramatic illustration of the gains for Downtown that they could achieve. Robert Harris co-chaired the committee that produced the first plan, the "Downtown Strategic Plan," which was unveiled in 1993. This plan originated in initiatives undertaken during Mayor Tom Bradley's administration (1973-93, especially by the LA 2000 task force, which began its work in 1989), and emphasized a newly-invigorated street life in the core, born of increased numbers of residents who would be attracted to move there by a renewed and more appealing cityscape. It emphasized connectivity among ten mixed-income Downtown neighborhoods and districts, establishing an improved pedestrian environment through the greening of streets and the expansion of open space and parks. It further proposed sixteen catalytic projects to create focused nodes in these districts. Not to be forgotten for his support of the Downtown Strategic Plan is developer Ira Yellin, a member of the plan's steering committee who died in September 2002. A passionate advocate of Downtown and its historic architecture, Yellin renovated key buildings that strengthened the plan's redevelopment nodes, including the Bradbury Building (1893), the Million Dollar Theater (1918), Grand Central Market (1987–1995), and Union Station (1939). A prime example of the plan's proposed interventions in the historic commercial district was the renovation of the Broadway Spring Arcade Building (1923). The seductive perspective drawing published in the plan showed a section through the arcade with renovated loft floors providing a live-work environment in the midst of historic buildings and theaters, transit networks, and nearby cultural activities. Carefully planned open spaces such as South Park Square, which gave prominent park frontage to the grand Mayan Theater (Morgan, Walls, and Clements, 1926), enhanced renovated and new buildings alike and increased residential prospects for Downtown.

Downtown developer Tom Gilmore, who arrived in Los Angeles in 1989, when the Downtown Strategic Plan committee began its work, has been both the beneficiary of their pictorial bible and the prophet of their dogma. From his company's offices in a sector he has christened the "Old Bank District," Gilmore works to replace housing that was lost in the razing of Bunker Hill and other Downtown neighborhoods with loft conversions of commercial structures. He practices what might be called "organic redevelopment," urban renewal that differs from that of an earlier era of master-planned redevelopment not only in its incremental approach, but also in the types of projects undertaken, which focus on infusing existing viable industrial and commercial districts with housing. He calls for "indigenous retail" and "full-spectrum housing," as well as the coherent, enlightened social policy planning that is necessary to achieve it. Yet he struggles to produce the legislated affordable housing quotas without the massive subsidies that were

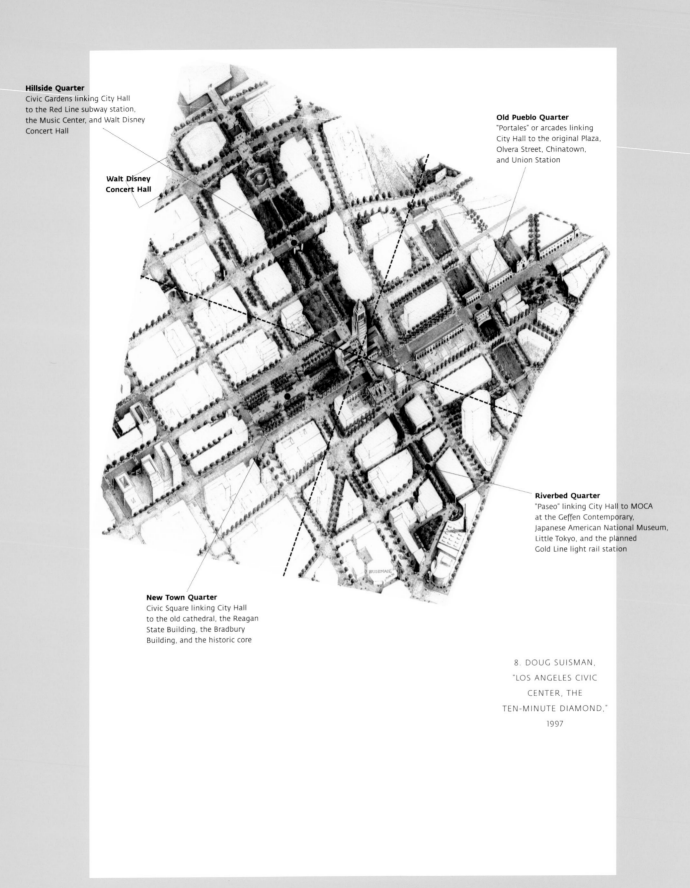

Hillside Quarter
Civic Gardens linking City Hall
to the Red Line subway station,
the Music Center, and Walt Disney
Concert Hall

**Walt Disney
Concert Hall**

Old Pueblo Quarter
"Portales" or arcades linking
City Hall to the original Plaza,
Olvera Street, Chinatown,
and Union Station

Riverbed Quarter
"Paseo" linking City Hall to MOCA
at the Geffen Contemporary,
Japanese American National Museum,
Little Tokyo, and the planned
Gold Line light rail station

New Town Quarter
Civic Square linking City Hall
to the old cathedral, the Reagan
State Building, the Bradbury
Building, and the historic core

8. DOUG SUISMAN,
"LOS ANGELES CIVIC
CENTER, THE
TEN-MINUTE DIAMOND,"
1997

at the CRA's disposal during the Silver Book era. If he is successful, his consuming dedication to the creation of residential space in the northeast quadrant of Downtown will transform that area, which may well become a model for other sectors of the core.

In 1995, during Richard Riordan's administration (1993-2001), the Civic Center Authority, which had been dormant since the 1980s, was revived and, perhaps inspired by the Downtown Strategic Plan, returned to an intense study of the heart of the heart of the city. This committee produced the "Civic Center Shared Facilities and Enhancement Plan," which the authority issued in 1997 (and reissued in 2000). Its crowning achievement was a richly visual document that relied on brilliantly concise and revelatory imagery to convey its vision and a "marketing" synopsis of sorts cleverly named the "Ten-Minute Diamond." Chief among the visionaries were Doug Suisman, architect and urban designer, who served on the consulting team, and Daniel A. Rosenfeld, who as the City's assets manager was conducting a study of City-owned real estate for the Department of General Services. The Ten-Minute Diamond forged a Civic Center zone of intensity and focus in which many of Downtown's most prominent public buildings and historic sites were located, providing nodes of intrinsic utility and interest to Angelenos and visitors alike (figure 8). It took City Hall as a compass point and drew an imaginary diamond-shaped perimeter around it, such that any point on that perimeter would be no more than a ten-minute walk from its rotunda. The *sine qua non* of the Ten-Minute Diamond plan was the creation of a system of variously designed open public spaces for pedestrians—linear garden paths—that encouraged habitation. It sectioned the Civic Center into four quadrants—Hillside, Old Pueblo, New Town, and Riverbed— and detailed what ought to be done to bring each into being. This idea of naming Downtown districts was a stroke of genius, since it created a framework for making places where, essential-ly, there were none. It was a corporate identity campaign for the body politic. Suddenly the city became knowable; the planners' goal, however, was not signage *per se* but signage used as a tool for sensitivity training. Cynically, one could make an analogy to the mapping of Disneyland— Main Street, Frontierland, Tomorrowland, Fantasyland—and Suisman acknowledged that he wor-ried about "coaxing reluctant imagery" from the city's history and its system of corridors.[10] Yet the Ten-Minute Diamond brought Downtown into relief, and with intelligent sincerity, countered what French sociologist Jean Baudrillard found in Los Angeles in 1986: "no intimacy or collectivity, no streets or facades, no centre or monuments...an extravaganza of indifference."[11] No longer.

The Ten-Minute Diamond clarified the locations where new projects of civic import might best be sited. The Caltrans District 7 Headquarters building—designed by Thom Mayne and his firm Morphosis—is rising on the block bounded by First, Second, Main, and Los Angeles streets, directly across from the site proposed in the plan (figure 9). Mayne diagonally juxtaposed the building to City Hall, incorporating into the design a public gathering space that enjoins the open-arms embrace of City Hall. The California Endowment's new headquarters, designed by Rios Associates, Inc., will articulate a neglected zone on Alameda Street between Union Station and City Hall in the Old Pueblo Quarter (figure 10). Anchoring the Riverbed Quarter, the proposed Children's Museum designed by Morphosis and the Central Avenue Art Park designed by Michael

10 Interview by author, 6 December 2002.

11 Jean Baudrillard, "America," in Neil Leach, ed., *Rethinking Architecture, a Reader in Cultural Theory* (London: Routledge, 1997), 224.

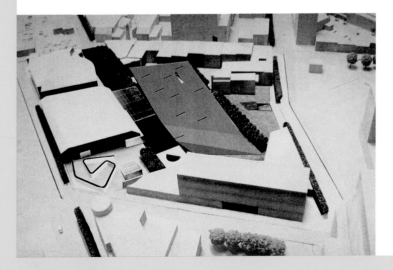

9. MORPHOSIS,
CALTRANS DISTRICT 7
HEADQUARTERS,
2003

10. RIOS ASSOCIATES,
CALIFORNIA ENDOWMENT
BUILDING, 2003

11. MICHAEL MALTZAN
ARCHITECTURE,
CENTRAL AVENUE ART
PARK, 2002

Maltzan (figure 11) would fill the block in which the Geffen Contemporary (a MOCA venue) and the Japanese American National Museum now float in a sea of parking lots. These new interventions would, in turn, create a transitional zone to the emerging Arts District near the Los Angeles River. Just outside the Ten-Minute Diamond, this more bohemian district—in contrast to the "high" cultural district atop Bunker Hill—is coalescing around the independent Southern California School of Architecture (SCI-Arc), which took up residence there in 2001 in a former freight depot. Architect and SCI-Arc director Eric Owen Moss and Dan Rosenfeld, currently principal of Urban Partners, LLC, which he co-founded with Ira Yellin, are contemplating the construction of housing, which would return a sense of urbanity to the area and involve the school as a key player in the development of Downtown.

Another major groundswell of revitalization at the edges of the Ten-Minute Diamond is the establishment of a new state park—as yet unnamed—in the area just north and east of Chinatown and Union Station, which the plan identifies as the Alameda District. Formerly known as the Cornfields, this thirty-acre parcel on the western bank of the Los Angeles River represents the triumphant acquisition in 2001 of open space for notoriously "park-poor" Los Angeles, which trails far behind other major American cities such as New York and San Francisco in the percentage of park land within the city limits. Led by the Friends of the Los Angeles River, which Lewis MacAdams founded in 1985, a consortium of activist organizations dedicated to the special cause of reclaiming the river along its fifty-eight-mile path through the metropolitan area achieved this landmark goal. From Charles Mulford Robinson's plan of 1909, which proposed to link the disparate sectors of the city by virtue of planted parkways, to the Ten-Minute Diamond of 1997, which made the heart of the city legible through the green weave of a Civic Garden and landscaped *paseos*, the purchase of the Cornfields marked the culmination of a century of movement toward a Downtown humanized by the interweaving of the built environment and parklands.

One of the largest contiguous metropolitan areas in the world, Los Angeles is immense. Its built fabric is ubiquitous. Given the sweep of the landscape across which Los Angeles spreads, any building that would have a fighting chance of contributing to a sense of urban identity must assume a powerful form equal to the staggering beauty of the conjunction of ocean, plain, and foothills. Downtown Los Angeles is visibly marked on the skyline by an impressive cluster of skyscrapers and clearly circled by a ring of intersecting freeways, so that, from afar, the center of the city is palpable. Within the heart of the city, however, this clarity and cohesion dissipate. Mindful of French philosopher Henri Lefebvre's assertion that urbanity demands a center, we can observe Angelenos struggling to promote a shared urban consciousness through the last century's failed or only partially successful attempts to create a strong image of the core.[12] The center is not only in need of landmarks, but also of sustained planning and building that will make it a place where the city's diverse population can live, work, and take their leisure. This is the socio-topographical imperative of Los Angeles, which Frank Gehry understands. It is also why Walt Disney Concert Hall is so important to Los Angeles, both

12 Henri Lefebvre, *Writings on Cities* (Oxford, England: Blackwell, 1996), 208.

as a singular monumental form and as a refractive lens through which the needs of Downtown are brought sharply into focus. Wrapped in raised gardens and balconies, the Concert Hall provides a dramatic podium for surveying Downtown Los Angeles and its breathtaking setting. Yet Gehry also believes in the power of civic architecture to strengthen human connections, not only to places, but also to one another. Gehry's desire that the Concert Hall be a "living room for the city" takes shape particularly in the billowing lobby so open to Grand Avenue, where passersby can stroll at will in and out during many hours of the day and night. In Los Angeles, Gehry has achieved the social diagram that he found compelling in his chief precedent for Walt Disney Concert Hall, Hans Scharoun's Berlin Philharmonie (1963): "It's a wonderful place to be because it puts people together and... engenders and encourages in some miraculous way a kind of interaction."[13]

13 Mildred Friedman, ed. Gehry Talks: Architecture + Process (New York: Rizzoli, 1999), n. p.

ANDREA VAN DE KAMP:

Disney Hall is a symbol of the city in the heart of the
city. Of those who have made contributions to Disney Hall,
one-third have given to support philharmonic music,
and two-thirds have given because they believe in Los Angeles.

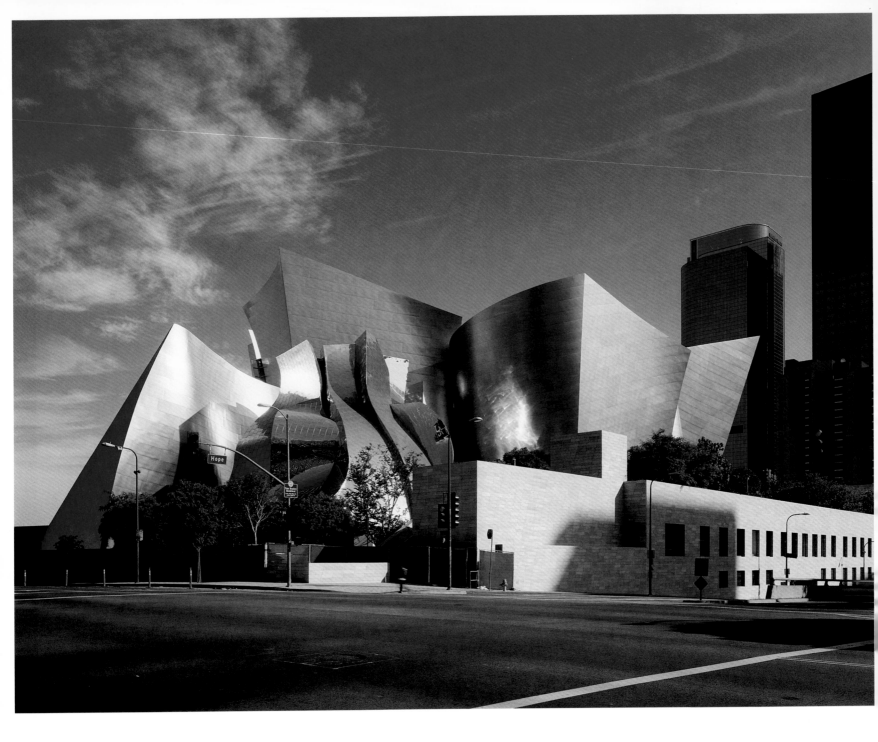

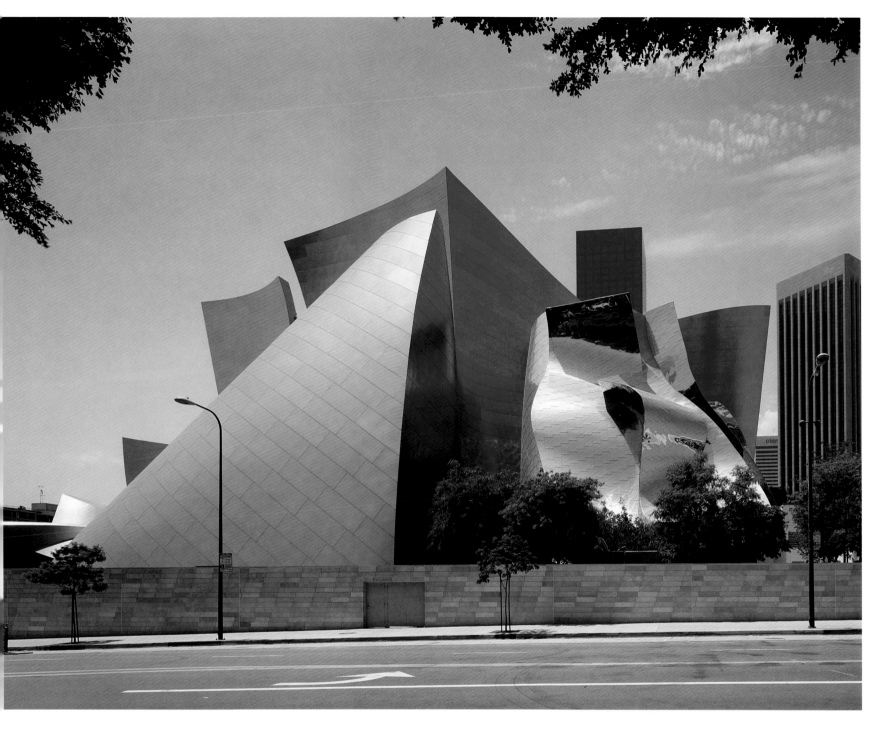

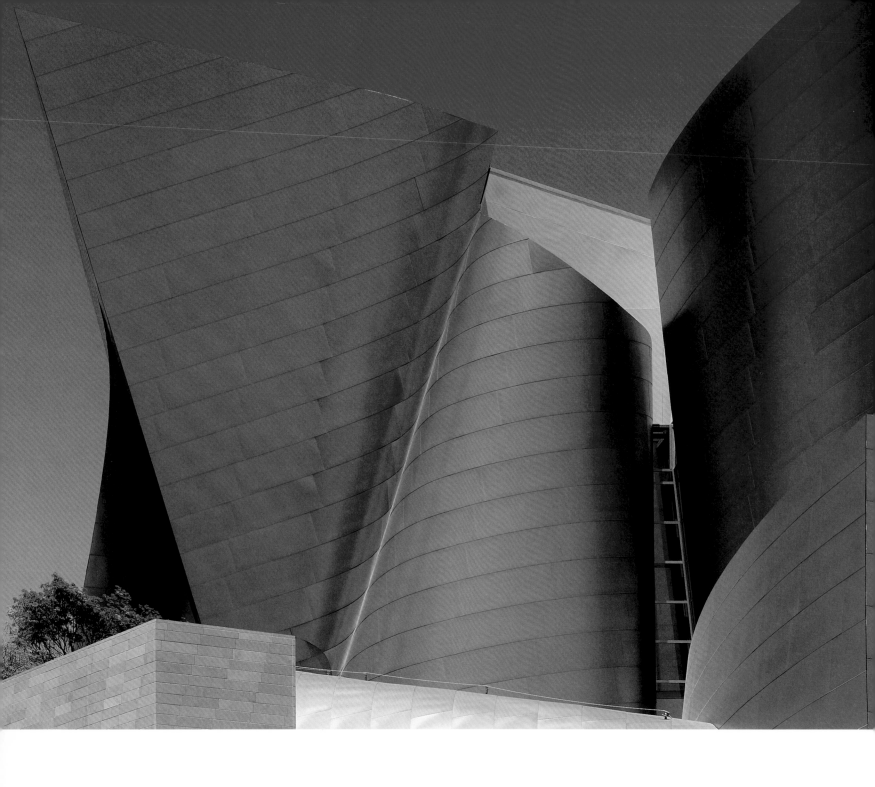

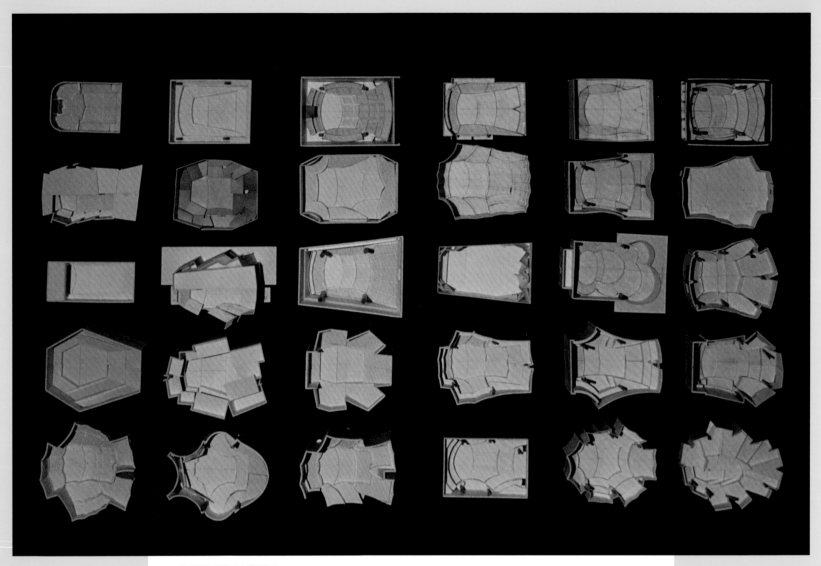

THIRTY SCALE MODELS
(ONE-SIXTH INCH TO ONE FOOT)
BUILT BY THE GEHRY OFFICE
IN 1989-1990 TO COMPARE
THEIR PROPOSALS
WITH EXISTING HALLS.
top left: CONCERTGEBOUW,
AMSTERDAM; center:
BOSTON SYMPHONY HALL;
bottom left: GEHRY
COMPETITION SCHEME

Michael Webb

A
Barge
with
Billowing
Sails

Fifteen years elapsed from the competition to the completion of Walt Disney Concert Hall, and the product of that extended period of creativity and delay is a masterly fusion of function, form, and feeling. Shimmering planes beckon from afar and draw you into a seamless complex of public and performance spaces. Stacked concourses and soaring volumes are cut away to admit natural light and to bring people together. They open onto gardens and vantage points from which you can contemplate the city. The building dances and sings, as though to prepare you for the experience of listening to music in an auditorium that is grand yet intimate.

Like all great works of art and architecture, Walt Disney Concert Hall has a quality of inevitability. You recognize a master's hand in the shifting compositions of steel and stone, the lyrical forms, and the organic flow of space. The building provokes surprise at every turn, delighting eyes and ears. And yet, everything you see and hear was the product, not just of a singular genius, but of a collaborative effort, one that involved contradictory recommendations and anguished revisions. No sooner had Frank Gehry's team won the competition than they returned to the drawing board to redesign the Concert Hall—first the auditorium, and then the exterior—from scratch. Had everyone rallied behind the project and the necessary funds been raised, the original design (or its immediate successor) could have been completed by 1993. The Los Angeles Philharmonic would have been delighted, and the world would have applauded, as it did when the Guggenheim Museum Bilbao opened in 1997. But the Concert Hall would have fallen far short—aesthetically and acoustically—of the masterpiece we have finally gained.

Civic boosters may regret that Bilbao got ahead of Los Angeles in claiming an icon as celebrated as the Eiffel Tower, the Golden Gate Bridge, or the Sydney Opera House. Over time, that setback will also come to seem insignificant. Painful as the ten-year delay was—for architects, music lovers, and the city's self esteem—it turned out for the best. The creative team was challenged to be more inventive, and it was accorded the luxury of time to resolve every issue and refine every detail. Gehry's mastery of a new architectural language and the acousticians' growing expertise raised Walt Disney Concert Hall to a higher plane of excellence.

The Guggenheim Museum Bilbao and Walt Disney Concert Hall share a curvilinear metallic skin, just as the Roman Pantheon and the New York Stock Exchange both have Corinthian porticoes, but they are radically different buildings. The museum creates its own site, stretching out to engage the Nervión River, a high-level bridge, and a backdrop of green hills. It is picturesquely massed, cellular, and tactile—its titanium scales seeming to flutter like leaves in a breeze. By contrast, the Concert Hall is taut, rigorous, and vertical in thrust. It builds to a climax, and is urban in character. It plays off the Music Center and the new Cathedral, the Department of Water and Power building; and the towers of Downtown: a gleaming centerpiece in the concrete jungle. It will win its own badge of fame.

Creating an inspiring symbol for the city was one of the imperatives of the project, but the auditorium was always the paramount concern. Ernest Fleischmann, the long-time managing director of the Los Angeles Philharmonic, defined the goal for the competing architects as "a single-purpose hall, a space where musicians and concertgoers will feel totally at home, and the audience will embrace the performers, [with] acoustics that are rich, clear, and warm." He felt that balconies and boxes reinforced a social hierarchy and proscenium arches separated players from listeners, and urged that they be eliminated. For him, the model hall—in its configuration and sound—was the Berlin Philharmonie, designed by Hans Scharoun in the early 1960s. He felt that it had "after two or three years of fine tuning and adjusting risers, developed an acoustic that comes near to my ideal for orchestral music—a rich, warm sound that preserves absolute clarity and transparency." He wanted no part of the current fashion for variable acoustics. "An acoustician should be able to get it right the first time," he declared. "I don't care to leave the hall to the whims of whoever is using it, or create a new profession of acoustic adjuster."

"The search for an acoustician was as important as the selection of an architect," recalls Fleischmann. He and his colleagues looked for someone with a proven track record and a willingness to work harmoniously with Gehry and not to dictate the design. They chose Dr. Minoru Nagata, whose firm had won acclaim for the acoustics of two Tokyo auditoria, Bunka Kaikan and Suntory Hall, and other Japanese performance spaces. Yasuhisa Toyota, who took over as head of Nagata Acoustics in 1994, recalls his first meeting with Gehry in Berlin—in February 1989—as a kind of blind date, with Fleischmann playing chaperon. "We were very nervous, but he was so friendly that we got along from the start, and went to a concert together at the Philharmonie," he recalls. "It impressed me as the work of a genius, but like Suntory Hall, it wasn't perfect; there were some dead spots."

It is fortunate that Gehry's team got off to such a good start with Nagata and Toyota, for the acousticians made it clear that, much as they admired the expansive plan of the Philharmonie and—by implication—the competition-winning design, they felt strongly that the shoebox plan and parallel walls of older European halls, like the Concertgebouw in Amsterdam and the Musikverein in Vienna, were better models. "Their recommendations were as different from those we had received in the competition [from another acoustician] as night is from day," recalls project designer Michael Maltzan. "We had plotted the sound reflections in two directions; Nagata did it in three dimensions, and he backed up his scientific analysis with a sensitivity to soft issues like psycho-acoustics." As Toyota noted, "acoustics is part technology, and partly dependent on our impression of the music, which is subjective."

Computers can tell you how much direct and reflected sound will reach every seat in the hall. However, some things cannot be measured precisely. Many people believe that the old halls sound good because they are made out of wood, a material that offers warmth and resonance, like the body of a cello. When musicians feel good about a hall it gives them confidence and they play better. Wood generates a feeling of intimacy and the audience becomes more connected to the music. However, Nagata discovered that the wood in the Concertgebouw was merely a decorative layer; it was the four inches of plaster underneath that enhanced the quality of the sound. That led to the decision to use only a thin layer of Douglas fir over the hard plaster walls and ceiling of the Concert Hall.

Size was a critical issue in the acoustics of the auditorium. It is much easier to achieve good quality sound in a small hall; unfortunately, the rising costs of live performance have pushed up the number of seats to levels that can defeat the best efforts of architects and acousticians. Boston's Symphony Hall (which was criticized for being too large when it was built in 1900) has 2,625 seats; the Dorothy Chandler Pavilion has nearly 3,100. Some of the Philharmonic executives would have liked to see as many as 3,000 seats in the new hall. Members of the orchestra preferred a ceiling of 1,800. Nagata opted for 2,000, as in Suntory Hall. Gehry's team struggled to reconcile the conflicting demands and found common ground in a final count of 2,265. The seats are steeply raked all around the performance area; as a result, the back row is the same distance to the podium as is the rear of the loge above the Founders Circle at the Dorothy Chandler Pavilion, and enjoys equally good sightlines.

The architects had to find out how much sculptural flexibility they had within the box, and they sought comments and advice from a wide range of musicians. Sometimes the response was blunt. Early in 1989, Gehry met with Sidney Weiss, the orchestra's then concert master, who told him: "We don't need an architect. The best concert hall is Boston. All we need is someone to go and measure it." Gehry learned that Weiss's hobby was copying classic violins, and at their next meeting said: "Sidney, I want to ask you one question: when you make a copy of a Stradivarius, does it sound like the real thing?" Weiss conceded the point and later observed: "We like to think acoustics are a science, but they remain a mystery. As with a great violin, you know it's good only after you play it. Frank loves music and is a great fan of the Philharmonic, so he was very open to suggestions."

Early in the design process, Gehry told Esa-Pekka Salonen, who was named music director in 1992, "I'm going to build models so that you can get inside my head, and you've got to respond." That launched an intense dialogue, in which Salonen became an important advisor and sounding board at every stage of the development. Models are Gehry's preferred design tools on every job, and only when he feels he has resolved all the key questions does he bring in the computer experts to scan the models and produce working drawings. His team made about forty models of existing auditoria and alternative plans for the Concert Hall, which gave the office a better understanding of the technical issues and built trust between them and Nagata Acoustics by providing a physical record of each move.

"We're trying to understand your principles so well that they will guide us as we draw and not let us make mistakes," Gehry advised Nagata. "We can interpret your ideas and make good architecture." Maltzan recalls that they "asked every question, from every angle, to check that there were no flaws in the acousticians' arguments.... Frank recognized that no matter how spectacular the building was, if the hall didn't work acoustically, it would be judged a failure."

Toyota recalls his "fantastic" experience working with Gehry: "Usually an architect has some image of the space and asks us, 'Please make it work acoustically'—that kind of process." Frank started from a completely blank paper [and] he integrated our acoustical request[s] or requirement[s] in the design."

Nagata's team tested the different configurations by modeling them in three dimensions on a computer. Calculations that had to be made mechanically over many hours on Suntory Hall in the early 1980s could now be completed in as little as five minutes, providing a rapid response to every proposal. However, as Toyota observes: "The computer is a powerful tool, but it can't do everything. We have to think about the physical properties of sound, which travels around physical barriers that block light." Tests were later performed on a one-tenth-scale model of the hall. Everything had to be reduced by the same amount, which required that the frequency of sounds be increased ten-fold to reduce the wavelength to a tenth of normal, and the model was filled with nitrogen to expel the oxygen and water vapor that absorb high-frequency sounds.

"It felt as though you were trying something new every day," Maltzan recalls of the model-making process. The designers were struggling to recapture the organic, sensual feel of the competition model and seeking ways to bring the audience and orchestra closer together. Gradually, their ideas coalesced around the concept of the seating deck as a sculptural form—what Gehry described as "a ceremonial barge." In essence, he fitted the vineyard layout of the Philharmonie into Nagata's box. The steeply banked tiers were partly inspired by Renaissance anatomy theaters in which the students stood within an inverted pyramid of narrow balconies to get as close as possible to the demonstration on stage.

In the Boston hall, the seats are narrow and tightly packed—to a degree that would not be permitted today. The goal for Walt Disney Concert Hall was to achieve the greatest density that comfort and safety would allow and to maximize exposure to direct and reflected sound on all sides of the stage. Not only would this enhance the sense of unity between the audience and the players, but it would give young concertgoers the visceral sense of music they have become accustomed to at rock concerts and by listening to music through earphones. The blocks of seating were broken up with low dividers to provide intimate groupings and early sound reflections, and the inner walls were tilted outwards to improve the acoustics and contribute to the dynamic quality of the hall. The balconies were kept shallow so as not to block the seats below from reflected sound.

The ceiling proved to be the most challenging part of the design. The acousticians wanted the hall to be made narrower, while the architects needed greater width to put more seats in the tiers on either side. The only way to get adequate sound reflection was to lower the ceiling, but this conflicted with the desire to bank the seats steeply. The height of the ceiling over the orchestra was set at fifty-two feet, but everything else was the product of discussion. "We would make a roof, they would analyze it, showing us print-outs of little red dots that represented the distribution of sound, and we would reconfigure it," Maltzan explains. The bowed strips of the ceiling, which evoke billowing sails, are precisely spaced and contoured to maximize sound reflection.

No feature of the hall better demonstrates the fusion of acoustical imperatives and architectural invention than the ceiling. The orchestra looks up to nine sensuously curved, inter-woven strips of wood veneer that suggest an abstraction of draperies in a traditional theater. They also recall the bent maple furniture that Gehry was creating for Knoll during the three-year

COMPETITION–WINNING

MODEL, 1988

MODEL MADE
TO EXPLORE EXTERIOR
WRAPPERS, APRIL 1991

SKETCH, MAY 1991

design of Walt Disney Concert Hall. The ceiling plays off the curved walls, and their Douglas fir surfaces complement the richer tone of the red oak floor in the auditorium. These woods were selected for their appearance, but the choice of Alaskan yellow cedar for the stage floor was determined by the need to achieve resonance. As Toyota notes, "the cello, double bass, and piano touch the floor directly, so the material, the thickness, and the structure below the floor (a resonating chamber) are important acoustically."

A similar concern to substitute sculptural form for applied ornament inspired the design of the 6,100-pipe organ. Gehry wanted to avoid the look of a church organ with its serried rows of metal tubes and created a dramatically splayed composition of hollow wood beams with technical assistance from Los Angeles organ designer Manuel Rosales. The organ was fabricated by the German company of Glatter-Goetz Orgelbau, and is the dominant feature of the auditorium. It will make its performance debut in the fall of 2004, following an extended period of voicing.

Natural light defines the perimeter of the room and provides a visual link with the natural world during daytime rehearsals and matinee performances. Nagata determined that the upper corners of the auditorium were acoustically insignificant, and that encouraged the architects to split open their barge to reveal a thirty-six-foot-tall window at the rear and a pair of skylights at each corner. In the Musikverein, as in other nineteenth-century halls, traffic noise penetrates the windows, but this was unacceptable in a hall that would be used for recording sessions. To ensure perfect soundproofing, the skylights are separate assemblies: steel boxes weighing nearly two tons each that were lowered in by helicopter. Outer windows of three-inch, and inner windows of two-inch-thick glass are set seven feet apart. The double-glazed north window is lined with sound-absorbing material.

The struggle to create sculptural form within the auditorium was replicated in the effort to find an appropriate configuration for the exterior. Gehry's competition entry differed from the others—as it did from the Dorothy Chandler Pavilion—in being designed pragmatically from the inside out, rather than trying to cram everything into a symmetrical container. The layout of the hall generated a sculptural form that could be rotated to the street grid and achieve a dynamic presence in the round rather than a static set of facades. The rotation freed up space for terraces and gardens, and provided an axial link south to the Museum of Contemporary Art, north to the Music Center, and east to a planned development of commercial towers. Gehry's victory was based in large measure on the way he addressed the city. "I'm trying to make a building that invites you in—the body language is welcoming," he explained to the Architectural Subcommittee. For the Philharmonic, that offered a friendlier image than the stiff and aloof Chandler Pavilion, and reinforced their efforts to reach out to attract a more diverse audience.

The competition entry included a chamber-music hall; later, a hotel and a ballroom were added to the program to generate revenue and foot traffic. At the end of 1990, it was decided that neither was economically feasible. This reduced overcrowding on the site, but left the rectilinear shell of the auditorium and a pre-concert lobby area as the only major interior spaces, along with an assortment of smaller rooms. Gehry and his team wrestled with the challenge of creating a fluid sculptural form that would unite these disparate elements. Project architect Craig Webb, who later succeeded Maltzan as project designer in 1995, played an important role in the creative process. "The problem of rotating a rectangular volume on an orthogonal site without making it look contrived was resolved when we came up with the idea of wrappers," he explains. Gehry began thinking of the wrapper as a mask that moves aside to reveal the hall, and that was the concept that was fleshed out over the next twelve months. Looking back, we can see it as a decisive moment in the architect's career, which led on to the Guggenheim Museum Bilbao and everything else that he has built or designed over the past decade.

The transformation in Gehry's language, from the direct expression of interior volumes as clustered orthogonal blocks to a layered composition of curvilinear planes, gathered momentum during the years the Concert Hall was taking shape, beginning with the Vitra Design Museum in Germany. Maltzan remembers the 1988 Vitra model as a seed that had an enormous impact. "Now, it would look dumpy; then it was a radioactive nugget—you were seeing the future." The Team Disney Building in Anaheim and the American Center in Paris, which were begun immediately after Vitra, are hybrids of orthogonal and curvilinear forms, restrained by the physical and economic difficulty of translating free-form sketches into buildable structures.

The breakthrough came in 1991 with Gehry's adoption of CATIA (Computer-Aided Three-dimensional Interactive Application), a computer program originally developed in France by the Dassault Systemes aviation company to design Mirage jet fighters, and subsequently distributed by IBM. It provided the architects with an essential tool, allowing them to scan models with a laser stylus and to feed the digitized information into a software program that could be used to draw, engineer, and construct the building. It's a two-way process, in which the software is first used to generate another model, which may be modified several times before the design is finalized. Computer files supplement the working drawings that are supplied to the contractors. CATIA was first employed on a metal fish sculpture that Gehry designed in 1989-92 for the Barcelona waterfront, and soon became an integral part of the design process.

Inspiration and technology went hand-in-hand. Gehry had always loved the sinuous form of the fish, and used it repeatedly as a leitmotif. Billowing sails were familiar to him—as a weekend sailor, and as an admirer of marine paintings by the Dutch master, Willem van de Velde. CATIA allowed him to abstract those forms on any scale and to compose walls of curved planes, using the software to direct the cutting tools and to make custom-shaped blocks of stone at an affordable price. Suddenly, Gehry felt as free as when he was in his boat, and his fluency in the new language grew rapidly. The sails took on a life of their own, as they do in the wind, and had to be tugged in and secured. For the study models, the architect used thin paper to express the movement and feeling of the forms, but quickly realized that "you can't have stone flying off into the air like a sail—it's not going to work." The curves echoed the billows in the auditorium and played off the bowed cornice of the Dorthy Chandler Pavilion, forging a link between new and old.

The possibility of cladding the sails in metal rather than stone had been considered as an economy measure as early as 1994, but Gehry resisted the idea, fearing it might remind Angelenos that he used chain-link and galvanized sheeting on his frugal early work. Despite winning the competition—and even today—his work enrages the Philistines. More importantly, there was the question of choosing the right material for the site. In Bilbao, a dip in the price of titanium had allowed him to use that costly material for the Guggenheim Museum, where it captured tonal shifts in the watery light of the Basque coast. He had used polished stainless steel for the riverfront façade of the Frederick Weisman Museum in Minneapolis, where its brilliance compensated for the cool northern light, especially in winter. In Southern California,

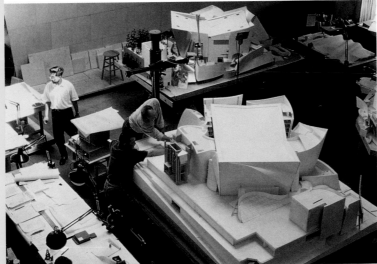

above: MODEL, EARLY 1992
left: STAFF IN GEHRY
PARTNERS' OFFICE WORKING
WITH MODELS,
SEPTEMBER 1993
below: ONE-TENTH-SCALE
MODEL PREPARED FOR
ACOUSTICAL TESTING

MODEL WITH METAL
EXTERIOR, DECEMBER 1994

CATIA COMPUTER
DRAWING OF THE STEEL
STRUCTURAL FRAME

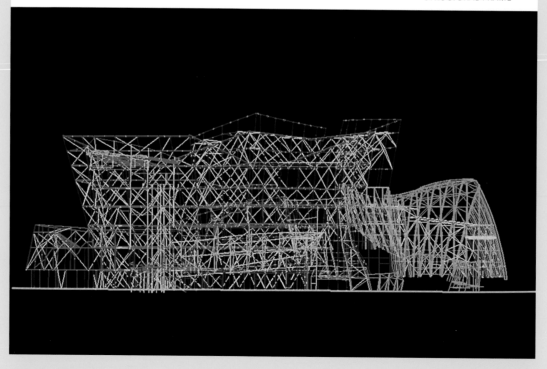

he felt the reflections from stainless steel would be too harsh, and at night, when the Concert Hall was in use, it was liable to appear dark. Limestone would be softer and warmer; also, as Webb recalls, "we were fascinated by the challenge of creating a fluid, dynamic architecture out of a dense and stable material."

In 1997, when the design process was restarted after a two-year shutdown, the new management committee estimated they could save at least ten million dollars by substituting steel for stone. The architects insisted that if the material were changed they would have to reconsider the sculptural forms. "To explore the issue, we clad the stone model with silver paper," says Webb, "and then we started changing and refining the shapes. As a result, the curves are stronger, less complex, and more refined. Stone would have had a limited number of compound curves; the steel has none. We spent longer on this than any other building we've done, and it shows."

The team decided to use rigid, three-sixteenths-inch-thick plates, wire-brushed in multiple directions to achieve a luster that would eliminate glare but remain luminous at night. They had used this angel-hair finish for a section of the Experience Music Project of 1995-2000 in Seattle, where the plates were brushed with an orbital sander by an artisan in Iowa to provide a rough, handmade quality that seemed appropriate for a museum dedicated to Jimi Hendrix. For the expansive planes of Walt Disney Concert Hall, refined, uniform tones and textures were needed, and the sub-contractor selected a Japanese firm, Nippon Steel, to fabricate and finish the 5,100 plates. To guarantee consistency, the coils were made from the same ladle of molten alloy and were run consecutively through the annealing mill before they were brushed in the same direction as they had been rolled. The plates were shipped to Los Angeles, where they were laser-cut, shaped, and given their edge trims. The wrapper was pulled five feet away from the box on the north side, to make the separation of outer and inner surfaces consistent all around. Two flights of steps that lead up from the street to the gardens are threaded through these interstitial spaces, in which you can view the structural frame that supports the sails.

For Lillian Disney, who was a passionate gardener, the plantings were almost as important as the building, and landscape designer Melinda Taylor, working with landscape architect Lawrence Moline, created a public park that doubles as a garden for concertgoers. Trees—including Chinese Pistache, Hong Kong Orchid, Pink Snowball, and Naked Coral—have been chosen to provide changing colors through the Philharmonic season and green shade in summer. Ground cover, designed to play a supporting role as well as attracting birds and bees, will spill over undulating beds onto travertine paving. Gehry added a flower-like fountain of fragmented blue tile, inspired by a piece of Delft pottery that Mrs. Disney cherished.

Within this garden, behind the stage of the Concert Hall, is an amphitheater that will be used for children's concerts and other open air events. A horseshoe wall of limestone blocks is wrapped around a six-level tier of concrete bleachers. A cantilevered steel canopy is faced with rounded plaster baffles designed to provide optimum sound deflection. The amphitheater is echoed in a belvedere looking out over the city, which is reached by a concave tier of concrete steps and enclosed by a steel wrapper.

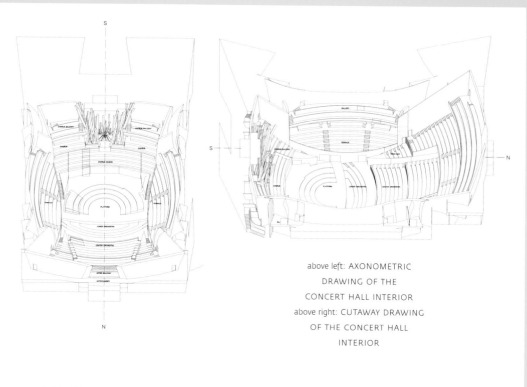

above left: AXONOMETRIC
DRAWING OF THE
CONCERT HALL INTERIOR
above right: CUTAWAY DRAWING
OF THE CONCERT HALL
INTERIOR

FINAL MODEL

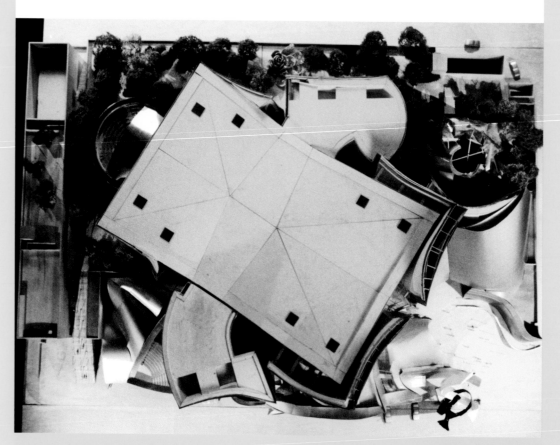

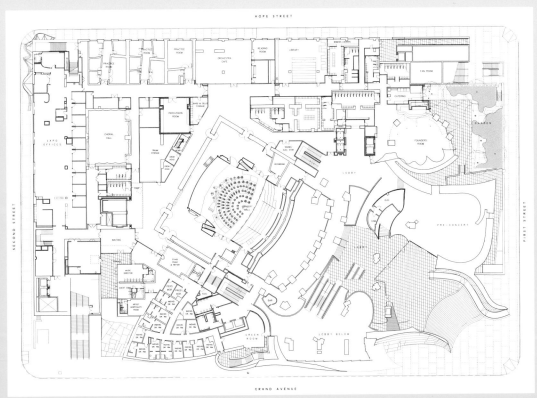

ORCHESTRA LEVEL PLAN

GARDEN LEVEL PLAN

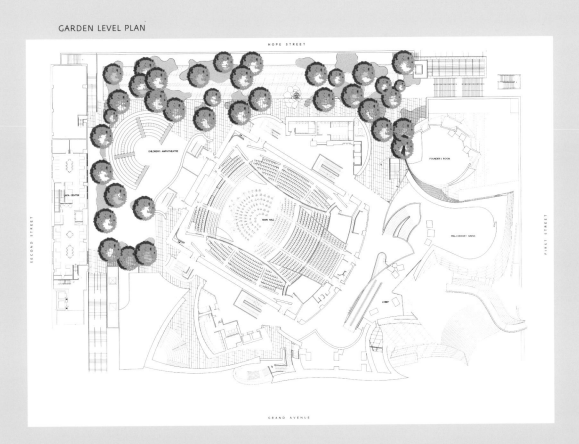

The boldly articulated Founders Room, located near the northeast corner of the site, had always been envisaged as a free-standing, steel-clad pavilion with a private, walled garden; now it was given a bright, annealed finish so that it would continue to stand out like an exuberant sculpture against the backdrop of the brushed steel sails. The architects borrowed from the Renaissance tradition of the double dome—pioneered by Brunelleschi in the Duomo of Florence—to simplify the steel structure and allow the plaster ceiling to have its own separate identity. Within this confined space, Gehry indulged his love of complex, interwoven forms that seem to be in motion. All the pent-up energy of his sketches is expressed in the scrolling, layered folds of plaster, which are modeled in light from above. Here, the fertility of invention is unconstrained, and Gehry acknowledges his debt to Borromini, the virtuouso architect of the Roman baroque, while exploring aesthetic and structural possibilities that Borromini could hardly have dreamed of.

If the Founders Room symbolizes the enlightened patronage of Los Angeles's establishment, REDCAT—a black-box auditorium and gallery—stands for experimentation. Located at the southwest corner of the building, its name is an acronym for the Roy and Edna Disney/CalArts Theater, and it gives the California Institute of the Arts, which Walt Disney founded, a long-desired presence in the heart of the city. The gift that made REDCAT possible arrived after the design of the Concert Hall had been finalized, so the architects had to find a place for it within the parking garage. A ribbon of the same bright annealed steel that clads the Founders Room wraps around the entrance canopy at the junction of Second and Hope streets. The gallery and theater open off a concourse that leads back to the garage. You enter the lofty auditorium at the middle level and step down to a bare concrete floor and loading dock in back. Hinged panels to either side swing open to provide additional points of entry and to dampen sound; a modular stage and raked seating for up to 266 can be reconfigured to suit any kind of production or projection. Executive Director Mark Murphy promises to make REDCAT a laboratory for challenging new work by local and international artists and performers.

During the two years, mid-1997 to 1999, that the rest of the building was being reshaped or tweaked, there was a strong feeling that the auditorium had found its final form and should not be altered. However, Nagata Acoustics had drawn on the Walt Disney Concert Hall model to shape the seating and sound in Sapporo Concert Hall, located on the northern island of Japan. Soon after its completion, in 1997, Esa-Pekka Salonen and Deborah Borda went to check it out, realizing that it would provide a foretaste of the Walt Disney Concert Hall. They were thrilled by the quality of the sound, and a visiting conductor, Simon Rattle, declared that it had the finest acoustics he had ever experienced. Ideas that Nagata had tried out for the first time in Sapporo were subsequently incorporated into the Concert Hall. Low walls were added close to the stage to balance direct and reflected sound in the front rows; upper balcony fronts were tilted down; and feathered articulation was added to wall surfaces as it had been in the ceiling.

The building program specified superb amenities for the Los Angeles Philharmonic musicians, who are scheduled to play one hundred and fifty concerts a year at the Concert Hall, and will—counting rehearsal time—spend more of their waking lives there than at home. Gehry provided a spacious green room, a library, a lounge, and

THREE PREPARATORY MODELS
OF THE FOUNDERS ROOM, 1998.
above: CEILING VAULT;
left: SKYLIT INTERIOR;
below: EXTERIOR WITH
STONE CLADDING

DRAWINGS,
above: RESTAURANT;
right: CAFÉ, BELZBERG
ARCHITECTS

practice rooms with windows looking out to Hope Street, as well as dressing rooms for soloists and ensembles, and storage areas for instruments to the rear of the stage. A gallery leads to the 150-seat Choral Hall, tucked in beneath the bleachers of the rooftop amphitheater, which may be used for public recitals and chamber music performances. The music director and guest conductors enjoy the use of a suite opening onto their own outdoor space. "I know of no concert hall where musicians have had such important input," says Fleischmann. Two floors of staff offices, with interiors designed by Chu+Gooding Architects, are ranged along Second Street and integrated with the backstage areas. These two wings, faced in staggered limestone blocks, serve as a podium from which the sails and treetops emerge where the hillside site drops away to the south and west.

Backstage areas are vital to the success of the Concert Hall and the productivity of the musicians, but the public will feel equally well served. In their competition entry, the Gehry team visualized the lobby as a transparent, light-filled "living room for the city," opening onto the sidewalk. In contrast to the tightly-enclosed foyer of the Dorothy Chandler Pavilion, the lobby would have a separate identity and serve as a symbolic bridge between everyday life and the inner sanctum. Walt Disney Concert Hall was intended to be a center of civic activity, not just a destination for concertgoers. People could walk in from Grand Avenue at the point where escalators emerged from the seven levels of the underground parking garage. They could explore the lobby, visit the shop or restaurant, buy tickets, enjoy an informal lunchtime concert, or stroll in the garden. It would be an oasis for local residents and office workers, for people on jury duty at the courthouse or taking in an exhibition at MOCA, besides serving foreign visitors who now wander dazedly through Downtown in search of something to see or do.

That enlightened concept has survived all the changes in design. Tucked in beneath the sails along Grand Avenue is a bifold glass wall that can be raised to open the lower level of the entrance lobby to the sidewalk, which has been widened and resurfaced to accommodate a witty sculpture by Claes Oldenburg and Coosje van Bruggen. At the corner of Grand and First is the main entrance, reached by a broad flight of steps paved with the same travertine as was used for the Spanish Steps in Rome. It evokes that baroque masterpiece in the swelling curves of the wrappers to either side, which part to reveal a tall window, and arch over the space named BP Hall to the right of the entry. Branching steel columns within the lobby are encased in wood to suggest a stylized glade of trees and draw the visitor's gaze to the skylights high above. Gehry acknowledged Lillian Disney's love of flowers in his design for the carpet—a stylized floral pattern that is carried through to the upholstered seats in the hall. The sensuously curved BP Hall is flooded with light from an elliptical glass ceiling. It accommodates up to six hundred people for daytime music-making, lectures, receptions, and educational programs. Though it is open to ambient sound from the lobby, its surfaces are treated like those of the auditorium, with a thin layer of Douglas fir (perforated at the lower level) over hard plaster on the walls, and a red oak floor to ensure a full, rich sound.

The café, designed by Hagy Belzberg who briefly worked with Gehry before establishing his own office, is tucked under the seating deck of the hall, and its tables spill out into the lobby. Patrons are silhouetted against two layers of translucent glass that is etched with bars and bathed in different colors of light. Belzberg also designed the gift shop to the south of the lobby, with display units that can be raised or lowered on stainless rods, and a restaurant that has its own canopied entrance on Grand Avenue. You enter the restaurant through a foyer that is defined by amber glass wine storage walls, and step into a room that pays homage, in its own distinctive way, to the fluid, curvilinear geometries of the hall. The carved walnut wall is an abstraction of a half-drawn curtain—evoking the beginning and ending of a performance—and the undulating white ceiling is modeled in amber light.

Construction of Walt Disney Concert Hall began in November 1999, and those who had waited over ten years for this moment, hardly daring to believe it would come, silently cheered as the steel rose skyward. Every piece was numbered and, thanks to CATIA, the shapes and joints were calculated to seven decimal points. Gil Garcetti, the former Los Angeles County District Attorney, documented the construction and got to know some of the ironworkers—129 men and one woman from Local 43. In his book, *Iron*, he quotes Johnny O'Kane, who said "Every ironworker likes a good challenge, and Frank Gehry throws an awfully good challenge."

Within nineteen months, the structural frame was complete and the sails began to emerge from the scaffolding, like a butterfly struggling free of its chrysalis. The cladding plates of stainless steel were taped to aluminum frames and clipped to aluminum channels that were attached to steel mullions. A three-inch cavity between the inner and outer layers serves for drainage and ventilation. Each plate fits snugly against a sliding batten strip and can be removed in eight minutes to provide access for maintenance. The sails appear to billow in two dimensions, but this is an illusion: each plate has a single curve. Within, the hall took shape as though this were a shipyard, where ribs and planks are laid on the keel of a yacht, and the deck and fittings follow, until it comes time to install the masts and unfurl the sails.

The auditorium is one of the world's great interiors, and it is likely to prove as impressive in terms of sound. In the final months of construction, the orchestra has been rehearsing in the hall and Toyota has been fine-tuning the acoustics, dampening the reverberations by adding sound-absorbent materials in the lattice panels set into the sides of the room and the ceiling pillows. The sound can also be varied by raising or lowering the hydraulic risers in the orchestra. It may take another year or more before the orchestra has learned to use the hall to full advantage, just as it takes time to play a new instrument as well as one with which you are familiar. Toyota discovered that the Tokyo orchestra was full of complaints about Suntory Hall before they adjusted to it, even as visiting musicians were extolling its qualities. Gehry has had ample time to reflect on what spells excellence. "After all this time," he says, "I've decided that it's one third acoustics, one third psycho-acoustics, and one third a great orchestra."

The Los Angeles Philharmonic has demonstrated how great it can sound during its guest engagements in the finest concert halls of other cities in the United States, Europe, and Japan. Now it can enjoy even higher standards on its home ground and welcome other orchestras to share its good fortune. Dedicated concertgoers are full of anticipation, but Walt Disney Concert Hall also has the potential to deepen public appreciation of serious music, anchor a burgeoning arts corridor, enhance the quality of life citywide, and reshape the image of Los Angeles around the world.

ESA-PEKKA SALONEN
AT THE CONSTRUCTION SITE
OF WALT DISNEY CONCERT HALL,
OCTOBER 2001

Esa-Pekka Salonen

Variations
and
Traditions:
CLASSICAL MUSIC
in the
TWENTY-FIRST CENTURY

For some time now I have awaited with great anticipation the completion of Walt Disney Concert Hall and the Los Angeles Philharmonic's move into its exciting new space. I see the Concert Hall as a bold symbol of the remarkable evolution the Los Angeles Philharmonic has undergone in the last several decades, and in many ways the new structure reflects the strengths of the Philharmonic as it exists today. Though deeply rooted in tradition, the Los Angeles Philharmonic has sought to break new ground in the presentation of classical music to contemporary audiences. In its innovation and elegance, Walt Disney Concert Hall will allow the Philharmonic to realize those goals more fully, and will be the perfect home for an orchestra that continues to look toward the future.

I first came to Los Angeles in 1984, when I was invited by then-managing director of the Los Angeles Philharmonic, Ernest Fleischmann, to conduct the orchestra on a guest engagement. Later, in 1989, when Ernest first approached me to become the music director of the Los Angeles Philharmonic, I knew that if I were to accept the position I would be surrounded by people whom I admired and whom I knew to be receptive to my ideas.

Several interesting aspects of the Philharmonic attracted me to the organization. Foremost, the orchestra itself was excellent and also had great potential. In particular, I was impressed by its multifaceted nature, including its openness to music of our time. In accepting the position as music director of the Los Angeles Philharmonic in 1992, I realized that I was inheriting something rich in tradition, with its own multi-layered, internalized memory that I had no intention of eradicating. Every conductor leaves his imprint on an orchestra, and that influence is reflected in the music. When I took over as conductor, though I had many ideas regarding the orchestra's future, I sought to build upon its tremendous heritage, not to react against it.

Before moving to Los Angeles, I had worked primarily in Europe and had little idea of what running an arts organization in the United States would entail. I realized soon after I took on my role with the Los Angeles Philharmonic that to lead an orchestra in the United States one must do much more than simply "make music," particularly since I chose to be the kind of music director who was not detached from the socio-cultural realities and dynamics of the society in which he lived. In running an American symphony orchestra, one is encouraged to consider carefully the exact nature of the orchestra and its role within the community, and then, naturally, to act upon those qualities.

There are many ways to judge an orchestra. One of the most obvious is, of course, the technical quality of the orchestra, its precision and unity of sound. In this sense, the Los Angeles Philharmonic ranks very high among the orchestras of the world, and I was confident in its abilities when I first accepted the position. Other qualities such as overall timbre, sound, level of energy, level of excitement, speed of reaction, and flexibility are more difficult to evaluate objectively because they fall within the realm of judgment. While these attributes are impossible to measure in any definitive manner, I believe that the Los Angeles Philharmonic now ranks very high in these areas, largely as a result of the conscious, focused work we have been doing over the last decade.

An orchestra is also distinguished by its repertoire and a willingness to explore new works. In this field the Los Angeles Philharmonic unquestionably stands out. A typical symphony orchestra, by definition, draws from a narrow segment of the entire tradition of Western music. If one understands this history as beginning with the theater of Ancient Greece and continuing to the present day, it encompasses well over two thousand years of music. Within this time span, we generally travel back a mere three hundred or so years for our repertoires. It seemed misguided, in my opinion, to continue to follow the path of most symphony orchestras by specializing even further within that already narrow slice of music history. In other words, instead of constructing a repertoire focused almost entirely on music from Beethoven to the late Romantic period, as many orchestras choose to do, I proposed that we distribute our emphasis more evenly among several periods. My view was that the most appropriate way to judge an orchestra was not necessarily only by how it plays Brahms, Beethoven, or Mahler, but also by how it plays John Adams, Steven Stucky, Magnus Lindberg, or Pierre Boulez. Ten years ago we set out to treat the entire program with an equal sense of adventure and sensitivity. We sought to open up the repertoire in such a way that no one specific period or area would be emphasized more than any other, a decision that has earned us a distinct reputation for innovation. In our current repertoire, if one were to identify the median year of all the works we now play per season, it would fall in the twentieth, rather than in the nineteenth century. Though we are still a century behind being "current," our shift forward chronologically has been (rather amazingly) regarded by many in the music world as a radical step.

It is astonishing how little relation there is between what is considered 'modern' in art and what is deemed 'modern' in music. Though the works of an artist like Matisse were perceived by many in the early twentieth century to be jarring and radical, those who view them today more likely find them completely appealing and fail to sense their original disruptive potential. With music, the situation is far different. For example, when one plays a less well-known piece by Stravinsky, a contemporary of Matisse, people today are likely to describe the music as "avant-garde" or perhaps "difficult," and to react not unlike many members of Stravinsky's initial audiences. Indeed, some music written in the 1910s and 1920s continues to have a frightening effect on people. This phenomenon is intriguing, and also somewhat perplexing, particularly when one considers that the sounds of contemporary rock or pop music are often far from "pleasant" or "pretty," yet they command a large audience of listeners. It seems that with classical music, in contrast, as soon as one steps outside the arena of "pleasant," one embarks on dangerous waters.

However, the situation in Los Angeles has changed and continues to change. Our audiences now are willing to be challenged. This was precisely our intention—to add an element of risk to the concert experience, and to demonstrate the benefits of experiencing the unexpected in a concert. This challenge is essential to our identity as an orchestra and forces us to operate on several levels to satisfy different needs.

The transition to a broader repertoire initially elicited a strong reaction, not only in the audience, but also in the orchestra. Many in the orchestra feared losing both our identity and the public's support. But soon it became obvious that by committing to these changes we were actually creating a distinct identity for the Los Angeles Philharmonic. We had been known as an "excellent orchestra" with "great sound" and "a lot of intensity," but we lacked any clear message of what qualities would distinguish us from other orchestras. Now, in contrast, the Los Angeles Philharmonic is known for its open-mindedness and versatility—its ability to move between styles and periods—a reputation we are certain to build upon and strengthen when we move into Walt Disney Concert Hall.

When I was considering the position of music director, I was enticed by the idea of leading an orchestra that would perform in a celebrated new concert hall that was both architecturally and acoustically ambitious in its design. I saw the decision by Los Angeles to build the new hall as an indication of the city's deep commitment to the Los Angeles Philharmonic, particularly given the many significant challenges a project of this nature in the Downtown area posed for all those involved. It was a bold and brave undertaking. At the time, I remember thinking how much I was going to enjoy being in a place where the spirit of Los Angeles was as strong as it appeared to be and where the people collectively supported such an exciting project.

Early into my tenure as music director, I spent several afternoons in Frank Gehry's office studying the very first architectural model of the Concert Hall he produced for the competition. That model, of course, hardly resembles the structure that is being built today. I soon realized that it was understood that the initial model would not necessarily reflect the final design, but instead would act as a starting point for it. Once Gehry had been chosen as the architect responsible for the building, the process of research really began.

It took Frank and myself some time to develop a close relationship, perhaps because we happen to have a similar temperament—a reticent, shy, northern manner. From the beginning, however, I was always amazed by Frank's openness to the concerns of the orchestra, and also by his overwhelming curiosity—about everything. I found working with him to be a constant source of excitement and inspiration. There was never a moment of vanity in his approach to this project; he kept the focus totally clear from the outset—the Concert Hall would be for the orchestra, for music, he assured us.

ESA-PEKKA SALONEN AND DEBORAH BORDA
AT THE PRESS CONFERENCE
ANNOUNCING THE INAUGURAL SEASON
AT WALT DISNEY CONCERT HALL,
NOVEMBER 11, 2002

from left: RY PRESSMAN, ARVIND MANOCHA,
EMMANUEL AX, AND ESA-PEKKA SALONEN
AT THE CONSTRUCTION SITE OF WALT
DISNEY CONCERT HALL, OCTOBER 2001

From early on in the project, I was involved in looking at models of some of the world's finest concert halls and considering how they would compare with Walt Disney Concert Hall. The architects even made a cardboard model of the concert hall where I used to work in Stockholm, the Berwald Hall of Swedish Radio, so I could compare that with the models of Frank's design during its various incarnations. I was fascinated by this process and interested in the models, because as a layperson, I was unable to read a three-dimensional image from an architectural drawing, just as I imagine a non-musician is incapable of reading a score and understanding how the music will sound. Without the skills to decipher these symbols, one cannot imagine the end product. To have these models in front of me and to be able to imagine the final structure more vividly was inspiring.

Much later in the process, Deborah Borda and I traveled to Sapporo, Japan, to visit the recently completed concert hall there. We were drawn to Sapporo because the hall—called Kitara—had earned a reputation as one of the best concert halls in the world and was a project of Nagata Associates. We wanted to learn how the concert hall worked in more practical terms, whether there were any problems we could avoid, and what it would be like to run the daily operations of a concert hall of that size and shape. We were also simply curious about the Kitara hall, given all the praise it had received from musicians. From the first moment we liked the design and found the sound to be absolutely fantastic. The experience was almost hallucinatory— the interior of the Kitara was so close to the design for Walt Disney Concert Hall that we felt we were stepping back into one of Frank's computer renderings that we had been studying for many years. We also saw how proud the local residents were of their concert hall, how beautifully the hall integrated into the landscape, and how well it functioned overall in practical terms.

Of course, our experience in Sapporo was valuable because in the end, the most important feature of a concert hall is the quality of its sound, though it is difficult to evaluate in objective terms. When one describes "good" sound, one often ends up in hopeless paradoxes, such as the assertion that a great concert hall has tremendous depth and warmth in its sound and yet is transparent at the same time. These attributes seem to contradict one another, but in fact, in a truly great concert hall, all this happens simultaneously. That is perhaps why language is often inadequate to describe these qualities. But if a musician perceives that the sound he or she produces resonates in an expressive way in the space, the musician is inspired to produce an even more beautiful sound. This loop becomes a flow phenomenon upon which the orchestra is carried away, resulting in a sensuous sound that is shared with the audience.

Even more difficult to describe is the feel of a concert hall. Some halls are cold, sterile, unexciting, and somehow fail to produce a communal experience. Others, such as the Philharmonie in Berlin, successfully create an intimate atmosphere. In such halls people are made to feel that they are participating in a communal ritual. Given the intimacy of the interior and the energy the design itself emanates, the concert experience in Walt Disney Concert Hall undoubtedly will be powerful. The hall is surprisingly shallow, and a dramatic view of the orchestra can be gained from every seat in the room. In addition, members of the audience will be able to see all fellow concert patrons, a rare feature in concert halls, and one that is certain to enhance the communal aspect of the experience. Those of us on stage will also sense the idea of communication more acutely than we do when we perform on a stage that is a separated from the audience. In other words, the most central aspect of performance—communication— will be emphasized by this new design.

ESA-PEKKA SALONEN
AND THE LOS ANGELES PHILHARMONIC
AT THE FIRST REHEARSAL IN
WALT DISNEY CONCERT HALL,
JUNE 30, 2003

LOS ANGELES PHILHARMONIC BOARD
PRESIDENT JOHN F. HOTCHKIS
CONGRATULATES ESA-PEKKA SALONEN
AND THE LOS ANGELES PHILHARMONIC
AT THE FIRST REHEARSAL IN
WALT DISNEY CONCERT HALL,
JUNE 30, 2003

I have derived great pleasure from the metaphors that Gehry has incorporated into the design of the Concert Hall. For me, even more powerful than the image of a boat is the idea of the interior of the hall as a floating unit within unlimited space. Gehry has described this interior as a type of sanctuary, and I think of the tiny slice of mankind—orchestra, conductor, audience—brought together here, floating in space, to share an experience, isolated from everything else going on in the world. In an age when technology seems to be rendering obsolete people's need to be together physically, such intimacy in a performance is essential. In my opinion, the growing alienation in society is dangerous for the human psyche, because I believe there is a biological need for collective rituals, for moments when a group of people in the same room concentrate on one thing, be it a religious service, a poetry reading, a concert, or any other experience.

A concert is a perfect ritual in this sense: The event is led by a master of ceremonies, people appear on stage dressed in traditional outfits, and the entire performance follows a ritualistic progression. To begin the performance, someone enters the hall and people clap, which, one might add, is an odd reaction. Regardless of the origin of this strange gesture, clapping remains part of the ritual and brings us together. When the orchestra then plays the music, people are prompted to witness collectively a powerful sensory and emotional/intellectual experience. As society becomes more fragmented in terms of geography, these types of shared rituals allow us to preserve an element of cohesion in our culture. For this very reason I believe that classical music performances will have a great future in our contemporary world.

In many ways, the delay in building Walt Disney Concert Hall worked to everyone's advantage. The transition to the new hall will draw more public attention now than it would have ten years ago, given the current international celebrity of Frank Gehry, along with my own longer experience as a conductor and composer. Most important, in the last decade the orchestra has developed in several ways and has continued to earn worldwide recognition for its achievements. The move to the new Concert Hall will provide a forum for everyone in Los Angeles to recognize what many in the music world have come to understand in recent years: that the Los Angeles Philharmonic is an incredible orchestra. In 1996, for example, after the orchestra traveled to Paris for a residence at the Théâtre du Châtelet, great reviews from around the world began to pour in. Suddenly there was a buzz surrounding the Los Angeles Philharmonic. It is perhaps one of the idiosyncrasies of Los Angeles that people often must earn their accolades abroad before they gain recognition at home.

The Los Angeles Philharmonic thus will move into the Concert Hall having established itself as an important orchestra globally and as a model organization in many ways, a model that other arts organizations look to as they initiate their own programs. In other words, there is a tremendous amount of interest in what we are doing, regardless of the new building. The Concert Hall, however, will help solidify the Los Angeles Philharmonic's position as one of the top-league orchestras of the world.

The miracle of Walt Disney Concert Hall is that there were enough people with courage to dream it up and actually see it through. Ernest Fleischmann, for one, never lost faith throughout the entire process. The project would not have succeeded had there not been the grass-roots and higher-level support in the city for both art forms—music and architecture. Now, of course, when I look at the Concert Hall as it nears completion, I realize how amazing the building is and how much it will add to the concert experience. By fostering more intimate communication through an innovative architectural design, the hall will allow the Los Angeles Philharmonic to push the entire art form of classical music forward in this city—and around the world.

Our challenge at the Los Angeles Philharmonic will be to show that classical music, orchestral music—which generally is not seen as the most dynamic of art forms but instead as more historically oriented—can be married with a radical architectural statement. When we move into the Concert Hall we must react to the challenge this new architectural and acoustical environment will pose and consider what will be the next step in the evolution of the orchestra. In our first season in the Concert Hall, we will preserve the Philharmonic's central legacy and tradition, but at the same time we will demonstrate new ways to look at the repertoire. We have created themes and mini-festivals for the season, and plan to promote ways of listening to music through the perspective of architecture; that is, to consider how music and architecture relate. In the future we hope to collaborate with members of the theatrical community and other artistic practices to find a new syntax or grammar of performance that will enhance the concert experience. We will also work to establish links with the community on a deeper level than before by collaborating with folk musicians, local community orchestras, jazz musicians, and perhaps some pop and rock musicians. As I see it, the Concert Hall will act as an open forum where one can expect to experience something out of the ordinary on every visit.

The gesture of constructing such bold architecture specifically for classical music will open many people's eyes and ears to the validity of a classical music experience in our culture today, which, we must recognize, is often still questioned. People ask, "Why do we listen to this old music written by dead people when we have all this exciting new stuff performed by rock and pop bands?" This is a legitimate question, but until now no one has seemed prepared to listen to an answer. Walt Disney Concert Hall will allow the Los Angeles Philharmonic to deliver its response to this challenge in an effective, compelling way. It will provide a more appropriate arena for the orchestra to pursue its ambitious goals for classical music and also to better serve a larger concert-going, classical-music-loving audience in Los Angeles. In the design for the Walt Disney Concert Hall, Frank Gehry has rethought the concept of the concert hall; he kept the essential traditional elements, such as the shape of the hall, while creating amazing variations surrounding the core legacy. This is our challenge: to keep alive the legacy of classical music, while at the same time rethinking music for the next century.

ACKNOWLEDGMENTS

Walt Disney Concert Hall is an
extraordinary project, realized through
the efforts of hundreds of people.
The following groups deserve special
recognition for their efforts:

The Disney Family
The County of Los Angeles
The Board and Staff of the Los Angeles
    Philharmonic Association
The Board and Staff of the Music Center
The City of Los Angeles

A special acknowledgment is extended
to all of the donors and corporate
partners who contributed to making
Walt Disney Concert Hall possible.

The editors of this book would like to gratefully
acknowledge the essential guidance of
Stephen D. Rountree and Arvind Manocha.
The Getty Research Institute and the
Getty Trust generously supported the photo-
graphic documentation of Walt Disney Concert
Hall and this book through the efforts of
Kurt W. Forster, Thomas Crow, Wim de Wit,
and Kathleen McDonnell. We would also like
to recognize the indispensable efforts of
Edward Burnell, Walt Disney Concert Hall Inc.,
Mortenson Construction, and Matt
Construction.

Thanks are due to photographer Grant Mudford
for his dedication to this project, along with
his assistant, Darrin Little. Finally, our deepest
gratitude to Lorraine Wild, for her talent
and her commitment, and to her design team
Jessica Fleischmann and Robert Ruehlman.

PROJECT TEAM

ARCHITECT
Gehry Partners, LLP

DESIGN PARTNER
Frank Gehry

PROJECT PARTNER
James Glymph

PROJECT MANAGER
Terry Bell

PROJECT ARCHITECTS
David Pakshong
William Childers
David Hardie
Kristin Woehl

PROJECT DESIGNER
Craig Webb

PROJECT TEAM
Andrew Alper
Suren Ambartsumyan
Larik Ararat
Kamran Ardalan
Herwig Baumgartner
Saffet Bekiroglu
Pejman Berjis
Rick Black
Kirk Blaschke
Tomaso Bradshaw
Earle Briggs
Zachary Burns
John Carter
Padraic Cassidy
Vartan Chalikian
Tina Chee
Rebeca Cotera
Jonathan Davis
Jim Dayton
Susannah Dickinson
Denise Disney
John Drezner
Nick Easton
Manoucher Eslami
Craig Gilbert
Jeff Guga
Vano Haritunians
James Jackson
Victoria Jenkins
Michael Jobes
Michael Kempf
Thomas Kim
Kurt Komraus

Gregory Kromhout
Naomi Langer
Meaghan Lloyd
Jacquine Lorange
Gary Lundberg
Michael Maltzan
Gerhard Mayer
Christopher Mazzier
Alex Meconi
Emilio Melgazo
George Metzger
Brent Miller
Julianna Morais
Rosemary Morris
Gaston Nogues
Jay Park
Diego Petrate
Whit Preston
Vytas Petrulis
Michael Resnic
David Rodriguez
Christopher Samuelian
Michael J. Sant
Michael Sedlacek
Robert Seelenbacher
Matthias Seufert
Dennis Shelden
Bruce Shepard
Tadao Shimizu
Rick Smith
Eva Sobesky
Suran Sumian
Randall Stout
Thomas Swanson
John Szlachta
Tensho Takemori
Laurence Tighe
Hiroshi Tokumaru
Karen Tom
Jose Catriel Tulian
Dane Twichell
William Ullman
Monica Valtierra-Day
Mok Wai Wan
Yu-Wen Wang
Eric Wegerbauer
Gretchen Werner
Adam Wheeler
Josh White
Tim Williams
Nora Wolin
Bryant Yeh
Brian Yoo
Brian Zamora

STRUCTURAL ENGINEER
John A. Martin & Associates, Inc.

MECHANICAL ENGINEERS
Cosentini Associates
Levine/Seegel Associates

ELECTRICAL ENGINEER
Frederick Russell Brown
& Associates

ACOUSTICAL CONSULTANTS
Nagata Acoustics, Inc. -
Minoru Nagata, Yasuhisa Toyota

**ACOUSTICAL ISOLATION
CONSULTANT**
Charles M. Salter Associates, Inc.

**THEATER CONSULTANT –
WALT DISNEY CONCERT HALL**
Theatre Projects Consultants

**THEATER CONSULTANT –
ROY & EDNA DISNEY
CAL ARTS THEATER (REDCAT)**
Fisher Dachs Associates

FIRE PROTECTION ENGINEERING
Rolf Jensen & Associates, Inc.

CIVIL ENGINEER
Psomas & Associates

ACCESSIBILITY CONSULTANT
Rolf Jensen & Associates

EXTERIOR WALL CONSULTANT
Gordon H. Smith Corporation

ELEVATOR CONSULTANT
Lerch-Bates North America, Inc.

**BUILDING MAINTENANCE
CONSULTANT**
Citadel Consulting, Inc.

GARDEN DESIGNER
Melinda Taylor Garden Design

LANDSCAPE ARCHITECT
Lawrence Reed Moline Ltd.

ORGAN DESIGN and FABRICATION
Rosales Organ Builders, Inc.
Glatter-Goetz Orgelbau

**GRAPHICS CONSULTANT –
WALT DISNEY CONCERT HALL**
Bruce Mau Design, Inc.

**GRAPHICS CONSULTANT –
ROY & EDNA DISNEY
CAL ARTS THEATER (REDCAT)**
Adams Morioka

LIGHTING CONSULTANT
L'Observatoire

WATERPROOFING CONSULTANT
D7 Group, Inc.

SECURITY CONSULTANT
Con-Tech Consultants

FOOD SERVICE CONSULTANT
Cini-Little International, Inc.

ENVIRONMENTAL MANAGEMENT
Sapphos Environmental

AUDIO CONSULTANT
Engineering Harmonics

HARDWARE CONSULTANT
Finish Hardware Technology

CONTRACTORS
Mortenson Construction
Matt Construction

OFFICE INTERIORS
Chu+Gooding Architects

**RESTAURANT, CAFÉ,
GIFTSHOP INTERIORS**
Belzberg Architects

AUTHORS

RICHARD KOSHALEK was chair of the Architectural Subcommittee for Walt Disney Concert Hall. He was director of the Museum of Contemporary Art, Los Angeles, for nearly twenty years. Koshalek is now president of Art Center College of Design, Pasadena, California.

DANA HUTT is director of Architectural Documentation and Special Projects at Art Center College of Design. Koshalek's most recent books include *At the End of the Century: One Hundred Years of Architecture* and, with Hutt and Thom Mayne, *L.A. Now, Volume One*, and *L.A. Now, Volume Two: Shaping a New Vision for Downtown Los Angeles: Seven Proposals*

GRANT MUDFORD is an internationally acclaimed architectural photographer. His photographs have been included in several museum exhibitions, most notably the retrospective on Louis I. Kahn organized by the Museum of Contemporary Art, Los Angeles. Mudford is represented by the Rosamund Felsen Galley, Santa Monica.

CAROL MCMICHAEL REESE is associate professor of architecture at Tulane University. Her books and articles focus on contemporary architecture and urban planning in the Americas. In 1985 Reese was commissioned by the Getty Research Institute to document the building of Walt Disney Concert Hall.

ESA-PEKKA SALONEN, composer and conductor, began his tenure as music director for the Los Angeles Philharmonic in 1992. At the Philharmonic, Salonen has conducted premieres of new works by many leading composers, as well as his own works. He has led critically acclaimed festivals and international tours. In addition to receiving the Siena Prize, Salonen has been awarded several medals: the Officier de l'Ordre des Arts et Lettres from France, the Literis & Artibus from the King of Sweden, and the Pro Finlandia from the Finnish government.

MICHAEL WEBB'S essays on architecture have appeared in numerous books and magazines in the United States and Europe. His most recent books are *Modernism Reborn: Mid-Century American Houses* and *Architecture+Design: LA*. He is the book review editor for the magazine *LA Architect*.

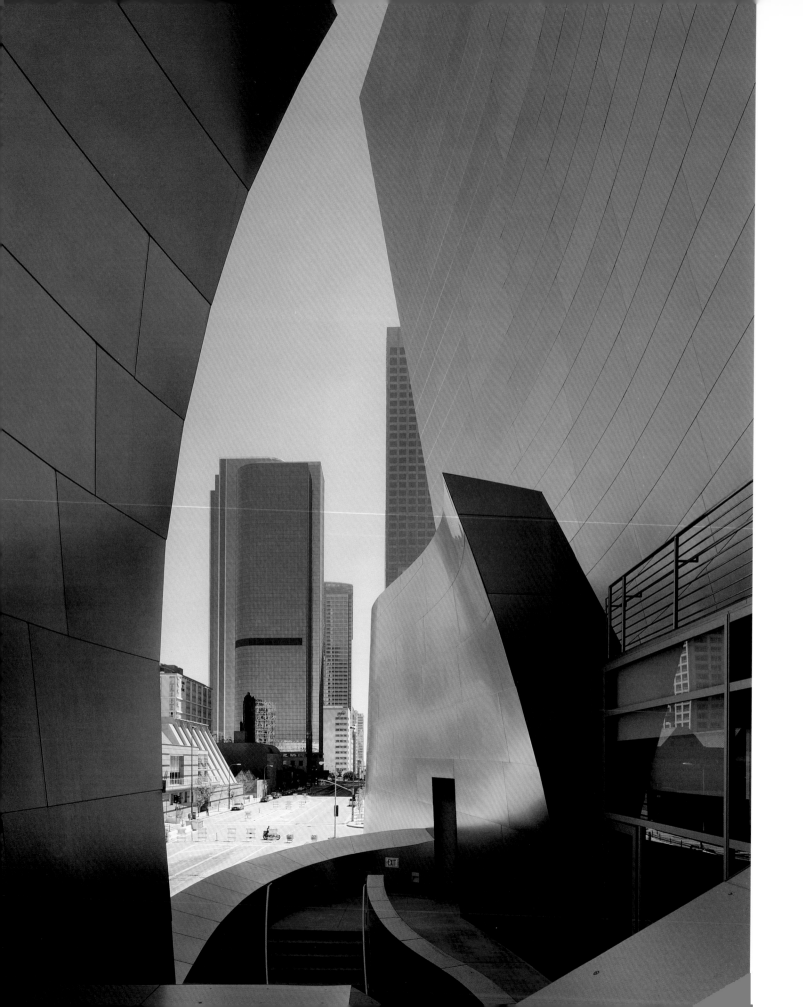

Individuals quoted in the essays by Richard Koshalek and Dana Hutt and Carol McMichael Reese were interviewed by the authors for this book.

ELI BROAD, founder of Kaufman Broad Home, SunAmerica Corporation, and the Broad Foundation, led the Walt Disney Concert Hall fundraising campaign after 1996.

ROBERT B. EGELSTON was chairman of the Music Center from 1993 to 1996, and is now a member of the Board of Directors of the Los Angeles Philharmonic.

ERNEST FLEISCHMANN was managing director of the Los Angeles Philharmonic from 1969 to 1998.

JAMES GLYMPH is a project partner of Gehry Partners and a project designer for Walt Disney Concert Hall.

RONALD GOTHER was the attorney for the Disney family and served on the Walt Disney Concert Hall Committee.

AYAHLUSHIM HAMMOND is project manager of the Bunker Hill Project Area, Community Redevelopment Agency (CRA).

ROBERT S. HARRIS is professor of architecture and urban design at the University of Southern California and chair of the committee that developed the Downtown Strategic Plan (1993).

JOHN KALISKI is an architect, urban planner, and principal of Urban Studio.

STUART M. KETCHUM developed the ARCO Plaza Towers (completed in 1972) and is a board member of the Music Center.

MICHAEL MALTZAN, principal, Michael Maltzan Architecture, was project designer for the competition phase of Walt Disney Concert Hall.

THOM MAYNE is an architect and principal of Morphosis.

DIANE DISNEY MILLER is the daughter of Walt and Lillian Disney.

FREDERICK M. NICHOLAS, attorney and real estate developer, was chair of the Walt Disney Concert Hall Committee for eight years.

STEPHEN D. ROUNTREE was appointed president and chief operating officer of the Music Center in 2002.

ANDREA VAN DE KAMP, chair of the Music Center Operating Board, 1996-2003, guided fundraising for the building of Walt Disney Concert Hall.

JOHN WALSH was director of the J. Paul Getty Museum from 1983 to 2002.

CRAIG WEBB is project designer for Walt Disney Concert Hall at Gehry Partners.

RICHARD WEINSTEIN was dean of the Graduate School of Architecture and Urban Planning, University of California, Los Angeles, from 1985 to 1994.

ZEV YAROSLAVSKY, Los Angeles City Council member from 1975 to 1994, was elected to the Los Angeles County Board of Supervisors in 1994.

IMAGE CREDITS AND COPYRIGHT

Unless otherwise noted, all photographs are by Grant Mudford, courtesy of the Los Angeles Philharmonic, and form a part of the photographic documentation commisioned by the Getty Research Institute.

p. 37 *left* courtesy of the Walt Disney Concert Hall Committee; *right* Courtesy of Diane Disney Miller

p. 43 courtesy of the Los Angeles Philharmonic

p. 45 photographs by Alex Berliner

p. 47 *top* courtesy of Frank Gehry; *bottom* photograph by Craig Schwartz

p. 51 photograph by Craig Schwartz

p. 54 courtesy of Thom Mayne and Morphosis

p. 56 courtesy of The Museum of Contemporary Art, Los Angeles; *bottom* photograph by Paula Goldman

p. 59 *top* courtesy of Yasuhisa Toyota; *bottom* photograph by Yasuhisa Toyota

pp. 60–61 photographs by Federico Zignani www.artdrive.org; courtesy of the Los Angeles Philharmonic, commisioned by the Getty Research Institute.

p. 70 courtesy of Gehry Partners

p. 72 reprinted from *Los Angeles, California: The City Beautiful* (Los Angeles: William J. Porter, 1909), n.p.

p. 75 *top* courtesy of the Department of Special Collections, Charles A. Young Research Library, University of California, Los Angeles, Allied Architects Association Collection; *bottom* photograph courtesy of I.K. Curtis, Inc.; www.ikcurtis.com

p. 76 courtesy of the Grand Avenue Committee

P. 79 courtesy of the Department of Special Collections, Charles A. Young Research Library, University of California, Los Angeles, Lloyd Wright Collection

p. 80 courtesy of the Grand Avenue Committee

p. 84 courtesy of Suisman Urban Design

p. 86 *top* courtesy of Morphosis; *center* courtesy of Rios Associates, Inc.; *bottom* courtesy of Michael Maltzan Architecture

p. 114 courtesy of Gehry Partners

p. 119 photograph © Tom Bonner

pp. 120, 123, 124, 126, 127, 129 courtesy of Gehry Partners

p. 130 *top and bottom* courtesy of Belzberg Architects

pp. 144, 148, 150 photographs by Federico Zignani, www.artdrive.org, courtesy of the Los Angeles Philharmonic, commisioned by the Getty Research Institute

Produced and edited by Gloria Gerace, Los Angeles,
and Garrett White, New York

Book design by Lorraine Wild, Los Angeles,
with Jessica Fleischmann and Robert Ruehlman

Text editors: Elizabeth Durst and Denise Bratton

Cover photographs: Grant Mudford

Printed by Blanchette Press, Vancouver, B.C., Canada

Library of Congress Control Number: 2003112419
ISBN 0-8109-4981-4 (cloth)
ISBN 0-8109-9122-5 (pbk)

Harry N. Abrams, Inc.
100 Fifth Avenue
New York, NY 10011
www.abramsbooks.com

Abrams is a subsidiary of